GLOBALIZATION
OR
DEMOCRACY

YOU CAN HAVE GLOBALISM OR DEMOCRACY, BUT YOU CANNOT HAVE BOTH

CLANCY HUGHES

2022

TABLE OF CONTENTS

INTRODUCTION

Globalism promised a one-world economy, which was to create such an overriding business prosperity as to end all wars. Globalization would bring competing nations into compliance with rules-based world trade and governing bodies such as the World Trade Organization (WTO). With success, however, came conflict and contradiction.

Following the success of the European Union (EU), the United States encouraged a more global loyalty, diversity, and inclusiveness. After the painful divisions of the Vietnam War, young people embraced globalism, traveling abroad in great numbers. Universities reformed curricula, teaching not only a more global view, but also a more diverse and inclusive view of history. A sense of idealism and one world came to dominate all levels of education and journalism, including our leadership and foreign policy. A young newspaper reporter stated, "I chose journalism to change the world."

Thus, globalism became a philosophy of free trade, international banking, world cooperation, and an idealistic sense of global citizenship, the notion embraced under a cloak of political correctness for the good of all mankind.

Globalization initially bought the Western world a new level of cooperation, openness, competition, and trade. Emerging from the war in Vietnam, the US sought a greater level of multilateral cooperation, international banking, and peace. We did so by contributing to an international bureaucracy dedicated to directing foreign policy and trade agreements with adversaries, hoping that the benefits of business and trade, even negative trade balances, would mitigate bad behavior. That strategy worked better with some than with others.

What then evolved, however, looked more like an oligarchy and an elitist shadow government undermining American democracy. Free trade sounded good, in theory, but globalism was not free, and the outcome was not good. We exported manufacturing and jobs with far more destructive consequences than even the skeptics had anticipated. Furthermore, China's Communist Party (CCP) and the People's Liberation Army (PLA) waged twenty years of "unrestricted warfare" against the US and the West with devastating economic consequences for the US, and America financed an accelerating growth and expansion for China.

Demonstrations erupted from the left in Davos and from the right with the Tea Party movement, and again with the populist election of 2016. What was prosperity in Washington was despair and stagnation on the street. And now, US tariffs and countermeasures led to even greater polarization.

The far left in one corner, and oligarchs in another, both look for power and advantage. The PLA spreads subversion and buys influence with politicians and educators, from the top right down to the local level. Seventy years of Russian ideological subversion plays out with race riots, conflagration, and chaos on American streets. How did this happen? What were the macroeconomic balances, and at what risk to America's democracy and freedom?

PART 1
CONFLICT AND
DEMORALIZATION

While rioters set fire to the streets of our cities, China conducts "unrestricted warfare" against America and the West, without firing a single shot.

CHAPTER 1. ONE WORLD

The fundamental structure of globalization grew out of Adam Smith's *Wealth of Nations.* Smith envisioned self-regulation by a magic hand of self-interest, and free movement of labor. Politically, Democrats embraced the division of labor and open borders, whereas Republicans embraced the magic hand of free enterprise, and cheap labor. History shows these principles to work well between contemporaries when the social order can limit corruption and greed—between states within the US or within the EU, for instance. Unregulated free enterprise distinguished America's corporate business structure. The ardor of deregulation redoubled with the fall of the Berlin Wall. Division of labor and free movement within the US and EU encouraged migration of labor to wherever it was most needed and specialization of production to wherever it was most efficient.

Globalization for the US in its present form, however, started with the Trilateral Commission (TC or TriComs) in 1973. David Rockefeller, president of the Council on Foreign Relations (CFR), together with Zbigniew Brzezinski and Jimmy Carter, organized the TC with the goal of economic cooperation, free trade, and a dream of one world, with cooperation, peace, international banking, and the furtherance of international government. Successes with the evolving EU encouraged the US to follow their example. Both the majority representation of foreign membership on the TC and publications by the CFR furthered the ideals of internationalism. This predominance of the commission's foreign leadership and policies directed by the CFR resulted in a substantial international influence on the US's own foreign and domestic policies.

Again, globalism promised universal prosperity, employment, improved living conditions, less poverty for underdeveloped countries, lower prices for higher-quality products, and eventual prosperity for all resulting from the efficiency of free trade. That promise had been reaffirmed repeatedly by economists, who asserted that the productivity and efficiencies from free trade, and free movement of labor and manufacturing (as initially described by Adam Smith) would benefit all participating countries. Economic models suggested that any transient loss of jobs or strategic manufacturing capacity would be more than compensated for by the improved efficiency of free markets. These beliefs were further embraced by competing US political parties; one, through the ideal of free trade and internationalism; and the other favoring the laissez-faire unrestricted free hand of self-interest, cheap labor, and the mantra of supply-side economics.

Furthermore, one cannot view the economics and idealism of globalization without considering the strategic and military implications. Failed and failing nations as well as territorial grabs pose very real threats to national security. Mitigating these risks with free trade at any cost had seemed cheaper than war. Unfortunately, for decades, the US bore the burden. Business and trade interdependence between nations, for a time, discouraged unwanted nationalistic expansionist forays. Economists, military strategists, young people, the media, and academia embraced globalization in solidarity.

I first met Vanessa Tompkins at a Rotary Club meeting where she gave a talk about her experience with import-export problems from China and Guatemala. Like most Americans who work for a living, Vanessa was highly networked and sensitive to customer needs and service. With a background in advertising at J. Walter Thompson in New York and IBM in Denver she was aware of the local economy and the growing distortions created by unbalanced trade. I was fascinated by her international trade experiences. Economics looks so different from the street. In 1982, Vanessa had started a "Buy American" campaign. Everything was made in Japan. It seemed a

5

simple thing to reenergize a nationwide Buy American imperative, as had been done in the past with union leadership. The initiative went surprisingly well. Red "Buy American" baseball caps and show-window-sized posters with local advertising drove a dramatic increase in Buick sales on Arapaho Road just down the road from Elway's Nissan dealership, reversing locally Buick's loss of sales to the Japanese car company. Consumers, even then, were aware of the problems with trade. They just had to be reminded. Rocky Mountain Buick was ecstatic and wanted to support and promote the campaign nationwide. However, corporate headquarters said, "Thanks, but the future is globalization and GM plans to lead the way."

CHAPTER 2. WHAT COULD POSSIBLY GO WRONG?

If you are a citizen of the World, you are a citizen of nowhere.

—THERESA MAY

The inescapable first realization that all was not well came with the loss of manufacturing, not just Buicks, but steel, coal, petroleum, washing machines, refrigerators, and soon nearly everything in sight. America's once strategic energy independence was all but lost to the Middle East. Think tanks, academics, and politicians told us we were no longer a manufacturing economy, rather a service economy. A former president said to the critics, "That horse is already out of the barn." Consumers would have told you that service was lost as well, however. The US loss of strategic capacity in favor of cheaper imports had more to do with cheap labor than with quality and efficiency. Asian manufacturing, subsidized by their own governments, soon exported such massive overproduction and underpricing as to shut out all competition.

In 2012 the US sold just 13,637 cars in Japan, less than Japan sold in a day in the US. Japanese cars accounted for 40% of the entire US market. Japan manufactured 10 million cars for a 5-million-car Japanese market. Japan listed no tariffs—as a bargaining chip—but practiced deep, shifting, impenetrable non-tariff barriers. The US collected 2.5% tariffs on Japanese cars and 25% on trucks. Two-thirds of the US trade deficit with Japan comes from automobiles.[1]

If the issue was just that of competition with foreign manufacturing, cheap labor, and imports, the US could probably hold its own, but US manufacturers themselves moved overseas for the cheap labor and a callously less regulated manufacturing environment.

China displaced the US as the world's leading manufacturer in 2010. Adjusted to 2005 prices from the UN database, between 2008 and 2016, Chinese growth in value-added manufacturing grew 94%; South Korea, 38%; Germany, 18%; France, 5%; the US, 3%; and Japan, 2%.[2]

By 2018 China's manufacturing output reached 2.01 trillion, US 1.867t, Japan 1.063t, Germany 700 billion, South Korea 372 billion.[3]

The five biggest US offshore manufacturers/importers were, not surprisingly: Apple, Nike, Cisco, IBM, and Wal-Mart[4].

In 1993 there were 355,000 manufacturing companies in the US. By 2011 the number fell to less than 259,000. American jobs, too, fell from 16 million to 10.26 million over the same time period. One in three jobs was lost between 1993 and 2011. Some portion of the loss resulted from the recession of 2008.[5]

Price Waterhouse Coopers cites the catalysts for US companies to return home as: economy, workforce quality, tax policies, regulatory environment, transportation, and energy costs. Darrell West at Brookings developed a scorecard on the above factors, including health, ranking countries on a scale of 100 for each country's ranking in manufacturing environment. No perfect score: UK and Switzerland 78; US 77; Japan, Canada, Netherlands 74. China scored 61 behind Germany, Spain, France, Poland, and Italy.

If globalization leads to the outsourcing of manufacturing, seeking cheap labor and less regulation, how could the US not believe that outsourcing of jobs would add to the problem of unemployment? In the idealized version of globalism, workers would leave their homes and move to the place where their talents were most appreciated. Underpaid skilled workers from Asia and elsewhere would move to America for better pay. Americans, however, are reluctant to leave the US for low-wage jobs in Asia, and herein lies the unanticipated tragedy of globalization, internationalism, and open borders. The outsourcing for cheap labor and unrestricted immigration for better pay, left US citizens with a continuing loss of manufacturing and jobs, and growing poverty.

A List of Problems

Humanitarian

1. Monopoly and greed here at home, as well as colonialism-like exploitation of rich foreign resources, cheap labor, and foreign markets, negate the expected efficiencies of globalism.

2. Depressed population, cynicism, poor health, and an increase in poverty are some unintended consequences of globalism.

3. Globalization does nothing for education, health care, or the environment.

4. Liberalization, and corruption of law and order on the street, drug addiction (and an absence of psychiatric hospitals) contribute to unsafe living conditions.

5. Years of neglecting public health; for instance, informed consent for HIV testing and confidentiality of results even within hospitals, unsafe water supply, and untested OTC drugs have made us vulnerable.

6. The outsourcing and cheap labor by technology has led to a revolution reminiscent of the Industrial Revolution.

Immigration

7. Disregard for US immigration laws favored the import of cheap labor, and political gain. The US excused massive caravans seeking opportunity through illegal entry. This, predictably, will only be the tip of the iceberg. The world's overpopulation already exceeds the world's food supply. Mass migrations seem a certainty.

8. Human trafficking brought indentured workers, prostitution, and slavery to the US.

Security

9. Outsourcing of manufacturing, loss of manufacturing capability, and strategic capacity became national security issues. You cannot have security with this level of outsourcing. You can only end up with the US forfeiting its strength to the benefit of those taking advantage of US grandiosity and naiveté.

10. New World Order resulted in wasted resources and lives, as well as trillions of dollars spent in the Middle East, with no real abatement of conflict and war. In some respects, nation-building policies made it worse.

11. The US has financed China's growth and military power without achieving the hoped-for collegial relations and rules-based enterprise between China and the free world.

12. Our foreign policy and the Machiavellian mandate to maintain a balance of power among adversaries have failed, specifically in the attempt to break up the old alliance between China, Russia, and North Korea.

Capital Divergence

13. Globalism leads to a concentration of wealth and poverty. Capital divergence is the unsustainable transfer of wealth to the top 1%. The transfer of wealth goes beyond the mere trade deficit. Investment capital grows many times faster than income, creating a multigenerational concentration of wealth. The concentration of wealth grows out of industry, technology, investment, excess profit, excess salary, and, to a major extent, globalization—hardly the magic hand of Adam Smith.

Investment Banking

14. Early globalization was about international banking. Commercial banks merged with investment banks, gaining a taxpayer protection (too big to fail). Furthermore, banks incorporated, ending their fiduciary responsibilities and community support. Extensive branch banking and big bank mergers stripped local communities of all local relationship banking.[6]

15. A stagnant US economy with minimal growth in GDP was sustained only by increasing the money supply. This boost in liquidity, however, was available only to the banks and big business with a usury level of high interest rates for the rest of America.

CCP/PLA

16. The SEC set aside stock market listing-qualification requirements, offering China a US market access for Chinese government-controlled corporations. This resulted in vast US financing of Chinese corporations and the Chinese military. These companies copied

directly from our own successful technology firms and built largely on stolen intellectual property.

Globalization became China's new term for Communist expansion and their own version of the New World Order: with theft of intellectual property, stolen military designs and specifications, cyber warfare, logistics, and geopolitical domination. See *Unrestricted Warfare.*[7]

17. We can blame China for an expanding drug problem with smuggled fentanyl, massive bribery, espionage, and subversion. We are vulnerable to generic drug imports from China, easily weaponized as already seen with the massive imports of fentanyl, and now with the Chinese pandemic.

Democracy

18. An overzealous rejection of American culture, institutions, values, mores, taboos, disregard for law and order, political polarization, and cultural conflicts within the US lead to a general impression that America is in decline.

19. A discounting of democracy and a drift toward oligarchy are among globalism's unintended results.

20. From the far left, we hear a cry for socialism, embracing the northern European model, cheered on by both Russian and Chinese ideological subversion.

21. In the US, a shadow government, an unelected worldly elite, promoted international interests above our own, dominating our foreign policy and our own democratically elected government.

Things went very wrong, but we continued because special interests made enormous profits, and the ideal of internationalism was so well entrenched among the so-called intellectual elite, academia, legislature, and the press, that nothing changed. Political polarization and hate prevented even rational debate of the issues. The concentration of wealth and unsustainable loss of liquidity from the middle-class and consumer market cannot last. Historically, this concentration of wealth has inevitably led to war, depression, revolution, and rarely, with the plague: "In death, all are equal."

CHAPTER 3. THE POISON APPLE

The division of labor among nations is that some specialize in winning and others in losing.

—EDWARDO GALLIANO

The ideal of globalization and free trade preceded even the writings of Adam Smith. With expanded trade and conquest driven by imperialism, the Roman Empire and colonialism sought one world order, often aided by slavery. Free trade found expression in fascism in the twentieth century. Why now the rejection of nationalism in favor of global citizenship?

The reinvented ideal of globalization today strives to end wars, foster world peace, promote multilateral cooperation, and achieve prosperity through regulated commerce and trade. Following World War I, the League of Nations was a start, and shortly after, in 1921, followed the CFR, and later, in 1973, the Trilateral Commission. These nongovernmental organizations (NGOs) achieved their goals beyond their fondest dreams, but there were questions and unforeseen outcomes. These organizers of trade and foreign policy that served America well initially, grew into to a shadow government, more international than constitutional or democratic.

The CFR, a nonprofit think tank, incorporated July 1921, publishes the bimonthly journal *Foreign Policy*. With 4,900 members, including practically all of the past bureaucracy, the so-called deep state, and an annual revenue of 101 million, its publications provide a virtual roadmap to US foreign policy. While much of CFR's direction has been positive, one must acknowledge that much of our foreign policy emanates from an unelected intellectual elite that, in practice, orchestrated US strategy, publishing in *Foreign Policy*, thus making transparent—and predictable—any subsequent US actions. When it comes to foreign policy, transparency is not a virtue.

Reaching far beyond the CFR, David Rockefeller, who was president of the CFR at that time, organized the initial meeting of the TC in 1973. The initial organizers were Rockefeller, Zbigniew Brzezinski, and Jimmy Carter, meeting to discuss global concerns and cooperation at a time when the European Union had already achieved many of these goals. The US sought cooperation between Europe, South America, Japan, and Asia, as well as securing cheap oil imports from the Middle East. The TC soon expanded to include European and Asian leaders as well as Canadian and South American.

Members of the Trilateral Commission, now often called TriComs, included virtually the entire cabinet of all subsequent administrations until the present. Familiar names include James Baker, Lawrence Eagleburger, George Shultz, Cyrus Vance, Alexander Haig, Henry Kissinger, Warren Christopher, and Harold Brown. Every administration, including President Obama's and President Obama himself, contributed to a philosophy of discouraging nationalism to foster business, banking, and government cooperation between Europe, North America, and Asia.

The TC allocates its 400-member votes as follows: 20 Canada; 13 Mexico; 87 US; 20 Germany; 18 for France, Italy, and the UK; 12 for Spain; and 1-6 for the rest of Europe, totaling 170 members. For Asia's 117 members: 75 Japan; 11 South Korea; 7 Australia and New Zealand; 9 for China, Hong Kong, Taiwan; and 15 for South east Asia including Thailand. Thus, the US holds about a 21% voice in an international organization whose policies strongly influenced virtually every administration from 1973 until the present (major cause of the bureaucratic sedition against the present administration—opinion).

During President Carter's presidential campaign in 1976, and his presidency, news media and opponents paid little attention to the influence of the TC. Former members of the commission made up virtually all the top positions in Carter's administration: vice-president, secretary of state, treasury, national security advisor, defense, and many others. Members were required to resign from the TC prior to assuming government office. This association held true for every administration, Democratic or Republican, up to and including the Obama administration. These unelected members of a shadow government, guided by international majority interests, constituted the decision-making backbone of every US administration, the left enamored by a sense of idealism and rejection of American institutions— a sentiment from the anti-Vietnam era—and the right by the advantages to international banking, cheap labor, profit, and "the new world order."

Senator Barry Goldwater wrote in his book *With No Apologies:* "In my view, the Trilateral Commission represents a skillful, coordinated effort to seize control and consolidate the four centers of power: political, monetary, intellectual, and ecclesiastical. All this is to be done in the interest of creating a more peaceful, more productive world community. What the Trilateralists truly intend is the creation of a worldwide economic power superior to the political governments of the nation-states involved. They believe the abundant materialism they propose to create will overwhelm existing differences. As managers and creators of the system, they will rule the future."

Acknowledging the strategic and security goals of stability through commerce and trade, the TC membership includes leaders from around the world, leaders whose interests are advanced at the expense of our economy and often to the benefit of international banking, and, as it turns out, the CCP.

The Commission, by its own mission statement, was trying to create a more liberal democracy and was concerned with educating and indoctrinating young people in a less nationalistic and more global view through schools, universities, the media, and churches, using perception management for a global view and behavior supportive of the goals of the TC.

One could argue that a political elite changed the fundamental American culture from one of Americanism, democracy, liberty, equality, the rule of law, and the Constitution to one of apology, rejection of American institutions, and a shift from nationalism to globalism, from one of semi-isolation to one of underwriting the economies and security for the rest of the world[8].

* * *

The unintended consequences of globalization were predicted by economic models, but not to anywhere near the extent that those consequences played out. The US began spiraling down, becoming a third-world country without the manufacturing, education, health, or financial strength to sustain its commitments: a condition strongly denied, even today, by the intellectual elite, including economists afraid to support the growing populist movement. America went from an economy in which one wage earner could support the family unit and educate its children to one in which all had to work, some at two or more jobs, childcare was neglected, and students borrowed money to pay for their own outrageous tuition.

Meanwhile, the media shroud the TC in a cloak of political correctness. And then there's China: championing globalization as their proxy for communism and their own version of a New World Order. Etcetera, etcetera. A chill Marxist breeze from the West.

CHAPTER 4. SEDUCTION

John F. Kennedy repeated, "A rising tide lifts all boats."

The aphorism works perfectly within the US or between equal trading partners. On a global scale, globalism's seductive song may raise the overall sea level, but not all seas, meaning not all nations, are equal in wealth, governance, productivity, or the rule of law. Of an 8-billion-person world population, 80% living on less than $10 per day had afforded manufacturers, fabless corporations, and oligarchs the perfect opportunity for exploitation. If globalization did cause rising tides, such a shift would drain successful nations in favor of corrupt and incompetent governments. Furthermore, America's ebb tide drained liquidity not from the wealth of government, banks, or manufacturers, but from the wealth of middle America, the consumer, the worker, and the taxpayer, and made rich the oligarchs and those exploiting the opportunity.

Despite the spectacular success of the EU and the spectacular strength of free trade among our 50 states, America's international globalization struggled from the start. Economists and policy planners failed to recognize and act upon the loss of liquidity and wealth among displaced workers, consumers, and the middle class. What developed looked more like the reemergence of colonialism with an exploitation of labor in underdeveloped countries and a drain on the liquidity of our own consumer market. Seduced by the promise of universal gain from globalization, the US suffered from the asymmetry of trading partners, unequal tides, and lost manufacturing. Multinational corporations, politicians negotiating the unbalanced trade,

18

investment banks, and foreign entities unwilling to play by the rules profited at the expense of the American people.

The outsourcing of both labor and manufacturing to the rest of the world created an unsustainable drain on the US and European economies. Economists wrote of these shortcomings, insisting that their models reflected these displacements, but that reeducation and adaptation would prevail and that in the long run, even in the midterm, all would benefit from the free movement and division of labor. Their siren continued with the argument that the US had failed to provide the necessary reeducation and entitlements for those hurt by globalism, but that in the long run all would so benefit from cheap consumer products that even those displaced would come out ahead. By the numbers, none of that optimism came to pass. Unemployment and closed factories led to mental illness, homelessness, and drugs. An opioid epidemic driven by prescription abuse and fentanyl exported from China led to demoralization, despondency, poverty, and death.

Massive waves and caravans of illegal immigrants attempted to overwhelm US borders, government, the rule of law, and the legal immigration system. Illegal open borders did not offer a division of labor as envisioned by Adam Smith's *Wealth of Nations.* However, the contentious cry for open borders did offer a gateway for criminals, subversives, and human traffickers, infiltrating ranks of refugees and children—not for work, where legitimate need attracts skilled migrants, but for organized crime and espionage—along with women and children seeking to take advantage of the opportunity to achieve entry into the US, legal or not.

Immigrants transferring earnings back home, and living off the grid, contributed to a drug culture and a further drain on both the tax base and US consumer market liquidity. Legal immigration of skilled workers, their families, and a certain number of refugees can strengthen our economy if assimilated, but not mass migrations. These shortfalls of globalization have been underestimated, overlooked, and deliberately ignored, often financed for deliberate subversion by the intelligence services of communist countries and sponsors of terrorism in the Middle East.

Cheap labor works for the supply side of the market up to a point; however, underpaid and underfed consumers do not do much for demand. It's all about supply and demand, a virtuous circle wherein supply and demand seek a sustainable balance. Draining income and liquidity from the buy side of the market changes the positive feedback loop into an unstable negative feedback. The resulting vicious circle leads to stagnation and deflation no matter how cheap the labor or how wealthy the supply side, but the seductive song of globalism goes on.

The trade deficit acts as a money pump, pouring consumer liquidity into the purchase of foreign goods and the profit of multinationals. Almost all consumer products, while cheaper, come from China, Japan, Germany, and all import costs from the sale of those products leaves the consumer side of the market. Thus, that consumer liquidity is gone. It does not, as before, turn over five or more times through other trades or purchases throughout the year. Yes, some—a diminishing amount, returns to the US as investment or represents the revenue for multinational corporations. Banks profit too, through foreign exchanges and investment back into the US, but the liquidity does not return to the consumer side of the market. Some foreign enterprise may engage in manufacturing within the US, offering added employment, but that's a small portion compared to lost liquidity on the front end. Although not the only factor in our maldistribution of wealth, our diminished trillions of USD lost because of the trade deficit, and most of our direct investments in Chinese corporations lead the pack.

Guilt, greed, political dogma, and ignorance drive denial. The media paint a rosy picture, philosophically committed to the status quo. "It's getting better, and overall we come out ahead with our free-trade deals," ignoring the trade deficit, the loss of manufacturing, and the capital divergence, all the while offering the lame excuse that the consumer benefits from cheap imports.

Political polarization may be as old as humankind. According to Victor Davis Hanson, polarity existed in 400BC Athens between liberty and equality. Our polarity centers more around taxation. The undercurrent may still be the polarity between liberty and equality just as in ancient Athens. One side would cut taxes to stimulate business and trade. The other side would raise tax on the wealthy. For generations, Keynesian economists argued with non-Keynesian economists over supply-side versus market-side forces as the driving force of the economy—which comes first, the chicken or the egg—adding to polarized thinking, both left and right, and not accomplishing much either way: two dimensions in a four-dimension world. A mule knows giddy-up, whoa, gee, and haw—four dimensions—but not our legislators, our economists, or the media living in a richly rewarding two-dimension gridlock.

Economists cling to a goal of fixing the problems, while continuing the same asymmetric trade policies. Politicians excuse the profiteering of big banks and multinationals, the disregard for US law and loyalties, favoring international allegiance with the ideal they still see as creating global economic growth and cooperation. The leadership holds out for the status quo, from which they gained power and profit. The so-called intellectual elite discourage nationalism and democracy in favor of international governance. Some demean the voter backlash as populism. Globalization is a belief system so ingrained in academic circles that economists make slanderous political statements to show their political loyalty before daring to question even the most obvious problems with its economic outcome. This kind of political expression begs academic and scientific credibility. Furthermore, the problems are not one-sided. Both political parties bear the blame for the problems and the responsibility for their solution.

Those who are doing well and those in the big coastal cities grow blind to the poverty, stagnation, and exploitation of the general population by a nouveau aristocracy. The globalists call the people's objections populism and neotribalism, all the while denying the very fundamentals of our democracy. Furthermore, gridlock and polarization dominate the economy as they do the political scene, a dangerous combination. This kind of political and economic polarization led to the American Revolution, the French Revolution, and our own Civil War. We suffered a massive recession triggered by the subprime housing crisis. In the slow recovery, we woke up to an appalling level of poverty, malnutrition, homelessness, illiteracy, poor health, a drug pandemic, violence, and incarceration rates on the level of a third-world country. Recent rioting and looting punctuate the eminent risk, and the extent to which foreign adversaries contribute to the chaos, loss of law and order, and defunding of our police. Was this a Russian-financed destabilization, Chinese, or did we do it to ourselves?

Intriguingly, this experiment in globalism resembles that of the Industrial Revolution (1760-1820). Our growth in poverty (called pauperism in 1795-1834) and our loss of a middle class resembles the English loss of a middle class, of independent freehold farmers, freeholders. Back then, new industrial countries suffered a staggering growth in population: 18% between 1811 and 1821, to which Malthus attributed poverty.

The stock market and the economy do not correlate. The stock market moves with a six-month anticipation of the economy and the increasing liquidity in the investor class, with some room for manipulation. The economy moves by liquidity too, mostly on the demand side, and the energy of buying and selling. The economy was doing well, with a way to go, when the Chinese pandemic struck. If we control the virus with vaccination and new antivirals, the economy may bounce back. However, it took forty-five years to drain the capital from the US population at large. The money supply still drives the Gross Domestic Product (GDP) along with supply-side

22

productivity, but not the energy on the consumer- and small-business side of the market. While much improved, the year-end 2019 GDP remains anemic. The income on the consumer side remains low in a long-term comparison. The Treasury's revenue December 2019 grew, year over, largely driven by customs and excise tax[9]—tariffs. Subtracting the tariffs, the Treasury's revenue was up 3% September 30, 2019 and 4.4% January 2, 2020 year over. Supply-side economic theory hopes that the increased productivity and added jobs from tax cuts will more than make up for the initial loss of tax revenue. We are not there yet. Our national debt increased, January 2, 2020 by 1.222 trillion year over. While good to celebrate the great economy and decreased unemployment, thus far, it amounts to only a drop in the bucket compared to the loss of consumer income, wealth, market liquidity, and the energy of turnover. The multiple in the GDP, while increasing, remained low—and then the pandemic.

All but ignored and certainly discounted, problems with free trade continue to mount up with frightening numbers. Political correctness protects this sacred cow of globalism and keeps the appalling trade deficit all but invisible; our education system advances the idealism of globalization and free trade as a given—a global community: "Think globally and act locally." Meanwhile, the multinationals and banks rake in the wealth. Ross Perot, 20 years ago, called it a giant sucking sound; however, his words went largely ignored. Back then, the trade deficit was at an eight-year record high of 114.23 billion; now more than five times greater, the trade deficit amounts to more than half a trillion dollars a year and growing. The trillions of dollars invested directly in Chinese corporations may be even greater. Was the US seduced by its own greed or did it have help?

CHAPTER 5. E=MC²

A nation is not made wealthy by the childish accumulation of shiny metals but is enriched by the economic prosperity of its people.

—ADAM SMITH

GDP does not allow for the health of our children, the quality of their education, or the joy of their play . . . It measures neither our wisdom nor our learning; neither our compassion nor our devotion to our country; it measures everything, in short, except that which makes life worthwhile.

—ROBERT KENNEDY

The GDP, a multiple, a fundamental measurement of economic activity, growth, and wealth, remains the most common measure of economic activity. Understanding GDP, however, requires understanding the multiples that generate the product, the turnover rate or velocity of the market multiplied by the money supply and the segment of the population to which it applies.

Einstein's equation relating mass to energy serves as a metaphor for understanding the power of market activity in driving the GDP: E equals money-supply, M; multiplied by velocity, C. The velocity of activity, C carries the greatest contribution, as in Einstein's equation.

Globalism, more than anything, must function within the framework of economics as it exists today. John Ise, the author's professor of economics, now deceased,[10] was all about supply, demand, liquidity, and marginal return. Ise also stressed the multiple in the GDP. He defined economics as the allocation of scarce means to alternative ends with the widest margin, marginal return, or diminishing returns, the elasticity of demand—or lack of doing so because there are a thousand reasons not to do what the numbers tell you to do. For instance: lack of understanding, political correctness, or a competing priority such as a pandemic or war. In any case, economics is the process we live by: our home, our business, our government, and all of those things combined. Tradition, common law, and politics define the framework of an economy, a framework of culture, of civilization—a means of cooperation and an insulation from the violence of a more primitive, no-holds-barred survival by tooth-and-claw existence.

Economists study this structure of cooperative interaction as political economics, historical economics, or statistical economics. Many, if not most, economists report their views, unfortunately, with a political bias. Historical data tell the more evidence-based story. The US Bureau of Economic Analysis (BEA) reports economic performance as GDP, often in terms of percent growth, and usually by quarter. Looking at only the percentages of growth or shrinkage can create a bias, however. The money supply multiplied by the turnover of money (economic activity, person to person, person to business etc.) defines the GDP, and the GDP is listed here by year and per capita. Per capita GDP distorts reality, however, because the maldistribution of wealth gives the wealthy most of the benefit while the wealthy contribute the least to the turnover of market liquidity.

Business and government look to the GDP as a measure of the strength of the economy. Gross Domestic Product, M1 x C, activity, or velocity = GDP, a product of circulating money multiplied by the number of times it changes hands in a given period of time, the velocity or turnover rate of domestic trade. The velocity or turnover reflects the energy and health of the economy; it has the greater impact on the product. No one pays much attention to the turnover rate. That's a mistake. That multiple correlates with productivity and that energy you feel on the street: liquidity times velocity, and that velocity correlates with people's current discretionary income, liquidity, productivity, and perception of the economy.

Energy may also better correlate with those things Kennedy said that GDP did not reflect—children's health, their education, the joy of their play and so forth—with optimism instead of depression.

The stock market and GDP correlate rather better with the wealthy's perception of the economy and with the supply side, while the multiple (velocity, turnover rate) correlates more with the people's experience.

Until recently, our GDP was flat; adjusted, it was in slow decline. Economic growth did not keep pace with population growth. For a simplified look at present reality, compare year by year the money supply expressed by the M1 with the GDP and the resulting calculation of velocity—a number not generally available. Note the dramatic drop in velocity in recent years despite an increase in money supply controlled by the Federal Reserve. December 2019 saw the GDP as growing. Note the drop-off with COVID 19 in the spring of 2020. The energy and market turnover increased in the first three quarters of 2019. It will be interesting to see if this growth will return. The turnover rate has a long way to go to achieve the numbers prior to 2008, however. The energy is still not there, and you can feel it on the street: depression, obesity, homelessness, drug addiction, crime, poverty, shootings, malnutrition, poor health, not to mention a loss of civility, rioting, looting, and a surprising number of people living in their cars.

GDP and Money Supply (M1) in trillions[11]

Date	GDP t	M1 t	(turnover) Velocity	Per Capita (GDP)
2019	21.54	3.9231	5.46	65623
2018	20.61	3.7277	5.53	62872
2017	19.39	3.5640	5.44	60035
2016	16.49	3.2446	5.08	57467
2015	16.47	3.0730	5.33	51486
2014	16.15	2.9212	5.53	50662
2013	15.76	2.6414	5.97	49849
2012	15.38	2.4586	6.26	49481
2011	15.19	2.1618	7.03	48775
2010	14.94	1.8600	8.03	48374
2009	14.54	1.6965	8.57	47576
2008	14.58	1.6034	9.09	49365
2007	14.99	1.3711	10.93	49980
2006	14.72	1.3849	10.63	49575
2005	14.37	1.3869	10.36	
2004	13.95	1.3900	10.04	
2003	13.53	1.3025	10.39	
2002	12.96	1.2187	10.63	
2001	12.71	1.1824	10.75	
2000	12.69	1.0896	11.65	
1999	12.32	1.1265	10.94	

1998	11.77	1.0916	10.78
1997	11.21	1.0714	10.46
1996	10.74	1.0707	10.03

Fig. 1. Note that the rising per capita GDP is interpreted as evidence of prosperity; however, per capita GDP is not uniformly experienced. With 40% of the wealth in the hands of the top 1%, this growth applies disproportionately to the wealthy, with increasing percentages of the money supply locked up in the hedge funds of the wealthy. A much better reflection of the economy for the average American is seen in the sustained fall in the turnover rate of money (the Velocity) from 10.93 in 2007 to 5.01 in 2018, now 5.49 as of October 2019.

* * *

I recall crossing the Irish Sea from Liverpool to Dublin in the late '80s. The contrast could not have been greater. The streets of Liverpool were dead, with a few misguided youths idling on street corners. Dublin was full of energy, crowded, with palpable energy—even young urchins attempting a pickpocket: the energy with which they fled across the plaza, thin print dresses flapping in the sunshine, reflected a joyful energy. Ireland, in a relatively short time, went from a depressed economy to one of the leading Western success stories, today with a huge trade surplus and a GDP growth of 23%. You can feel the energy on the street—it's a reflection of the velocity of money, turnover rate, the multiple in the GDP. You can see the same progress in Ireland's health care, leading the western world in quality by the same statistics that rank the US 34th.

—THE AUTHOR

The adjusted GDP showed a slow decline until 2017. The striking increase in M1 money supply since 2010 reflects Janet Yellen's credit easing in an attempt to stimulate the GDP/economy. Sadly, the banks as the primary recipients of the added liquidity, loaned to small business and consumers at high interest rates, if at all. The low prime-interest rates had gone to big business and secure mortgages. Low interest rates were good for big business, not so much for the consumer (12–24% credit cards) Any attempt to stimulate the economy must work both sides of the equation: Money X Velocity = GDP. Any economic stimulant must include the demand side of the market.

Demand. $\triangleq$ Supply

The Fed is limited in its ability to stimulate the economy with low interest rates. You can't go much lower than zero. The Fed can go only so far in printing money or credit easing and should look instead, or additionally, to velocity. Vitalize discretionary income and productivity, but on the consumer side of the market. The biggest missed opportunity was the subprime mortgage crisis. During the Bush administration, investment banks managed to get a law passed eliminating bankruptcy protection for homeowners and student loan recipients, setting the stage for the massive sale of subprime mortgages, student loans, and yet another banking crisis—the third in a generation. Fraudulent (opinion) loans were foreclosed; the bankers having sold the mortgages got rich, and the end mortgage holders, the big investment banks, were bailed out by the taxpayer. The missed opportunity was for the end mortgage holder (big banks and hedge funds) to take the hit, declaring the mortgages invalid and thus (1) allowing the homeowners to remain in their homes; and (2) realizing a windfall gain from the canceled mortgages returning massive liquidity to the consumer market, where it would soon be spent again and again, creating more of the much-needed liquidity and turnover.

> *The money was all appropriated for the top in the hopes that it would trickle down to the needy. Mr. Hoover didn't know that money trickled up. Give it to the people at the bottom and the people at the top will have it before night, anyhow. But it will at least have passed through the poor fellow's hands.*
>
> —*WILL ROGERS*

This harsh strategy would have first punished the banker's Ponzi scheme, and second, sent an infusion of capital, taken from the ill gains of the mortgage brokers and banks, back into the consumer side of the market. Third, such a strategy would have preserved housing for many of the 3.4 million now living on the street and working off the grid, if at all, because their paychecks would be garnisheed by the banks if they were to file a W2.

We can paint the same story for student debt, including dropouts with high debt: no way to pay it back, no bankruptcy relief, and no employment—not even counted as unemployed. Any employment results in garnishment of wages, thus any earnings remain off the grid while they're living at a parent's home or on the street as an escape. If the government were to cancel the debt, or reinstate the option for bankruptcy relief, it would (1) allow the indebted students to work—that's pure productivity; and (2), put "energy" back onto the street, and yes, at the expense of the debt holder, but many weren't getting paid anyway. Another bailout paid by taxpayers would not be productive. It's all about supply and demand, liquidity on the consumer side of the market, a liquidity lost by the highly profitable trade deficit, lost jobs, and lost manufacturing.

A number worth following for investment purposes is the Daily Treasury Statement, which lists the Treasury's revenue by day, by month to date, and by year to date. The two-day percent growth year-over tends to correlate rather closely with short-term stock market movement. In a sense, that number represents a proxy for the available discretionary income of investors, stock market investor liquidity. (It may reflect consumer market liquidity as well—purely conjecture.)

In 1992, few people were willing to acknowledge the loss of American wealth, more often reported as a spectacular wealth of a few. When Ross Perot on the election trail lectured on the loss of wealth, the media hardly noticed, but instead carried out a campaign of character assassination.

Vanessa Tompkins later said that she had joined the Ross Perot (1930-2019) presidential campaign of 1992. Perot placed educational commercials depicting the tragedy of outsourced jobs and wasteful spending. Perot found equal support from the Bush and Clinton supporters and especially from independents and moderates. In June, Perot led both Bush and Clinton with favorable Gallup poll numbers of 39%. He did well in the debates but became reclusive over threats from the media to sabotage his daughter's wedding. Perot's "giant sucking sound" describing the trade deficit, remains his lasting legacy. Ross was a Naval Academy graduate, serving in the navy 8 years before working for IBM and later starting Electronic Data Systems (EDS); he later financed Steve Jobs's computer company, NEXT, a company Jobs started after leaving Apple. Perot also famously staged a daring rescue and overland escape for two of his employees jailed in Tehran by Iran's Revolutionary Guard in 1979. Vanessa said she was disappointed by the lost opportunity to stop the drain on jobs, manufacturing, and liquidity back in 1992 and went on to other things.

Tracing the unforeseen consequences of globalism involves multiple interwoven threads. Gaining any quantitative, statistical, or proven facts eludes all but the best of our statistical and historical economists. The political correctness of globalism in institutions of higher learning and in the "deep state," if we were to define the entrenched bureaucracy as such, silences political economists; they are not talking for fear of their reputations, their tenure, their students, and their jobs.

Fifty years of Cold War and the war in Vietnam led to a liberal rejection of American institutions, favoring international interests and a new world order less sympathetic to the welfare of our own citizens. Additionally, the accumulated 40% of our wealth in the hands of the top 1% of our population[12], with 100 trillion US total worth[13] —resembled the monarchies and aristocracy preceding the Industrial Revolution and the American Revolution, with a sequestration of capital unavailable to the consumer market. The most sacred cow, however, remains globalization, with a trade deficit of 800 billion a year eroding our domestic liquidity and wealth. A lost wealth that is in no way replenished by direct foreign investment or mitigated by low-cost imports. Every purchase of imported goods amounts to a negative entry to our GDP, relative to the actual amount paid to the foreign exporter.

Furthermore, the increased money supply, engineered by the Fed, went to the banks to lend, not to the people or to small business, but to favored customers. The banks make more money with high credit card interest and investment banking than in affordable consumer loans and relationship banking. "To give it to the people," as one economist said, "you would have to drop it from a helicopter." The recent rapid growth and resurgence of US manufacturing and small business will go a long way toward fueling the discretionary liquidity on the consumer side, but the ongoing drain on market liquidity remains unsustainable, further inhibiting the velocity (multiple) and our quality of life.

CHAPTER 6. CAPITAL DIVERGENCE

An end to US trade deficits? That's not something trade policy can or should deliver.14

—*PAUL KRUGMAN*

Beyond lost manufacturing and jobs and beyond imported poverty, the middle class all but disappeared with a transfer of the near limitless wealth from the American consumer to the trade deficit, foreign entities, the investment banks, and to multinationals.

Economists point to the accounting reality that trade deficits are in US dollars, creating investment worldwide, creating growth far greater than the loss with much of the money reinvested back into the US. They point to the Sectoral Balances equation by Godley and Cripps, a formula taught in first-year economics where S = domestic savings; m = imports; x = exports; I = investments; g = government spending and t = treasury revenue:

$$\overrightarrow{Liquidity}$$

$$\mathbf{S + (m\text{-}x) = I + (g\text{-}t)}^{15}$$

The formula economists refer to shows a balanced accounting, wherein money lost from trade deficits and consumer savings goes to investments, government spending, or treasury. The formula does not quantify whose investment, whose government, or whose treasury. If you think about it, the equation more exactly reflects the flow of liquidity from the left side of the equation to the right, a flow of money and wealth out of circulation, out of

33

the hands of most American people and into supply-side profit, much of it foreign, and to sequestered assets. The capital lost in the trade deficit goes to foreign profit, foreign government, and a little of it returns as foreign direct investment in US bonds, equities, businesses, and property: assets built on the lost liquidity and wealth of the American people.

Globalization thus led to the worst outcome of all, capital divergence. We are left with an extreme sequestration of wealth in the hands of a small plutocracy of investment bankers, executives of multinational corporations, politicians, overpaid media, overpaid athletes, and a few professionals, at the expense of—and the exploitation of the rest of the population. Globalization brings us a new form of pillage and plunder, not only exploiting foreign labor in many of the poorer countries that were supposed to benefit from globalization, but also our own labor force and citizens in what has been called the virtual disappearance of our middle class.

The fact that capital (wealth) grows four to six times faster than income over time creates a problem for both capitalism and democracy.[16] Capital accumulation over time builds at the expense of the purchasing power of the consumer market, leading to depression—arguably the basis for long-term economic cycles. The extreme accumulation of wealth among fewer and fewer people threatens democracy with oligarchy—now a global problem. Intriguingly, this extreme concentration of wealth correlates not just with depressions but with wars, famines, and pandemics.

The problems with unbalanced trade were evident from the start— some that predated globalization and some that globalization made worse. The preponderance of Japanese imports, especially automobiles, had prompted debates between those pointing out the trade deficit as unsustainable and economists who insisted that the overall equation remained balanced and in the long run the efficiencies of free trade would benefit all trading partners. The economists won the debates, insisting that foreign profits resulting from the trade deficit came back to the US as investments, thus returning wealth and employment.

Economists' models identified the displacement of workers, but assumed adaptation, retraining, cheaper imports, and government support would minimize the downside. However, liquidity drain on the consumer side of the US domestic market amounted to $12.256 trillion lost in trade since 1975[17]. This loss had accrued from the trade deficit alone and represented a loss of wealth from the consumer side of the market. Economists excuse this loss as a balanced gain to others, which, of course, it was.

Far more than the calculated loss in economic models, the loss in wealth added to the reduced income from the outsourcing of jobs and manufacturing. Outsourcing of US jobs led to massive displacement, unemployment, depression, and poverty. Furthermore, the loss of income bled further the loss of liquidity from the consumer side of the market. The loss of wealth had resulted in a loss of the middle class (reminiscent of the loss of middle-class freehold yeomen farmers during the Industrial Revolution) [18]. Both Adam Smith and Arnold Toynbee cautioned that the benefits from unrestricted free trade did not apply in all cases.[9] Our gratuitous promotion of unbalanced trade to discourage bad behavior and promote trade had taken a heavier-than-anticipated toll on our own workers and consumer market liquidity.

After World War II, the Marshall Plan rebuilt Germany and much of Europe, as well as Japan. The US was an economic juggernaut. We could afford it back then, but that extreme industrial and consumer wealth had been long gone as we promoted deficit trade agreements in the new century. The question: Did these trade agreements reduce bad behavior by totalitarian regimes or merely finance further expansionism?

Instead of saying, "An end to US trade deficits is not something trade policy can or should deliver," economists might better say, strengthen our human factors, security and productivity, to more fairly compete and block those unwilling to play by the rules of free trade.

Despite the hope that globalization, and the American sacrifice it entailed, would end wars and bad behavior, the opposite appears to be the case. The doctrine of the New World Order, if anything, promoted more fighting, and attempts at nation building led to multicultural incompatibilities. The cost was incalculable in lives and unsustainable in the trillions of dollars.

Historically, the Civil war cost 498,332 lives; World War I cost 116,516; World War II cost 405,399; Korea 54,244; Vietnam 90,220; and since 9/11, wars have taken 6,852 lives. Since 9/11 there were 52,010 wounded in action, many of whom would have died but for our advanced battlefield medicine and evacuation. The death toll, however, does not account for traumatic brain injuries, TBI, or posttraumatic stress disorder (PTSD), and 970,000 VA disabilities. (In perspective, the Covid19 pandemic has cost over 200,000 US lives in its first 9 months). According to a Brown University study, the dollar cost since 9/11 exceeded $5.9 trillion, others say $7 trillion.[19]

Meanwhile, China financed its own development with the proceeds of America's unbalanced trade and our direct investment in unaudited Chinese corporations. Furthermore, the CCP aggressively orchestrated predatory trade practices with theft of trade secrets, now cyber warfare, and subtle Chinese-style bribery of US leadership right down to the local level. All threatening our national security.

While our government engages in political infighting, short-term market profit, greed, monopoly, and personal power, China makes long-term subsidized and strategic development projects in a new hybrid form of market communism. Take for example China's Silk Road, rail, and economic development project based on strategic long-term economic-political-expansionist goals. The struggle between democratic laissez-faire capitalism and authoritarian market communism will likely continue on the Chinese-driven economic playing field of globalization and weaponized information technology if we do not respond decisively to the threat.

Congress has little or no ability to manage economic systems in its present level of gridlock, yet it remains quite successful at undermining the executive function of our government. Not just in our current political climate but going all the way back to Lincoln's administration. The effort to thwart executive power did not end with the 22nd amendment. Limiting the president to two terms upset the separation of powers among the three branches of US government, giving the administration even less ability to manage crises outside political gridlock. Simply put, neither the judicial nor the legislative branches have the capacity to lead an economic struggle against an authoritarian communistic market-directed adversary. Such a response demands decisive leadership as written in the Constitution.

While China extends its influence and success, paid for by our own middle class, the propaganda machine of political correctness fights over the controls of our economy in the name of globalization. China has turned globalism into a new front of communism—not perhaps the initial intent, but taking full advantage of its cheap labor, the high level of advanced education we provided their students, and the ease with which they can assimilate our technology, provided almost willingly by US manufacturers outsourcing both manufacturing and labor. If Boeing manufactures a 737 in China—or even uses a cell phone, it gives the Chinese hackers access to the design characteristics, not just for the 737, but for the specifications and designs of all Boeing's military aircraft. Whether by partnership, required technology transfer, or cyber warfare, the US underwrote China's education, technology, manufacturing, military weapons systems, and financed it all.

China now finds itself in the enviable position of dominating all levels of manufacturing, leading in artificial intelligence (AI), database mining, fifth generation mobile network (5G[20]), logistics, cyber warfare, and a questionable accounting of wealth—with a population of 1.3 billion.[21] (Is the CCP secretly printing money and cooking the books with unearned credit balances, aside from and unknown to the accounting of international monetary systems?)

PART 2
DEVELOPMENTS AND
DESTABILIZATION

CHAPTER 7. HISTORY

The problem with political economists is they live so well that they have no knowledge of business on the street.

—THE AUTHOR

Every generation rewrites the past, but in times of danger, we are driven to the written record by a pressing need to find answers to the riddles of today.

—JOHN DOS PASSOS, The Ground We Stand On

Economists tend to fall into three groups: political economists, statistical economists concerned with the actual numbers of market behavior, and historical economists concerned with evidence-based outcome: inductive logic from historical analysis. Economics was not new to the twentieth century; indeed, it's as old as human interaction. The story begins with mercantilism, a class structure in which the monarchy and the nobility accumulate gold by colonialism, pillage and plunder, a highly positive balance of trade. The nobility and the church exercised what little social contract then existed, distributing a minimum of relief to the masses by *noblesse oblige* and by way of the church. Revolution, farming, and land ownership brought about a change.

The late 18th century saw a perfect storm of change from the American Revolution, the French Revolution, Adam Smith's book *The Wealth of Nations,* and the Industrial Revolution, which led to population growth, overcrowding, poverty, and in Europe, Marxism. In the Americas, free land and cheap natural resources led to its own industrial boom, capitalism competing with an agrarian economy and slavery, leading to a civil war.

Historical Economists

Under Capitalism, the more money you have, the easier it is to make money, and the less money you have, the harder. Wherever there is great prosperity, there is great inequality. The affluence of the rich supposes the indulgence of the many.

—ADAM SMITH

Adam Smith (1723 – 1790) was the epitome of the absent-minded professor: introverted and deeply analytical, he exhibited unusual habits of speech, gait, and facial expression, talked to himself since childhood, painting a familiar persona of semi-autism. Smith was born in the county of Fife, Scotland. His father, a senior solicitor and judge advocate, died two months after Adam was born. Raised by his mother, Smith never married but he enjoyed a close friendship with his academic and intellectual associations. Entering the University of Glasgow at age 14, Adam studied moral philosophy, graduated in 1740 at age 17, and entered graduate studies at Balliol College, Oxford with a scholarship. In 1751 Smith earned a professorship at Glasgow; he published *The Theory of Moral Sentiments* in 1759, a morality based on empathy, earning a professorship at Oxford. Smith began public lectures in 1774.

In 1763 Smith left his prestigious professorship at Oxford for twice the pay to tutor the nephew of Charles Townshend; in that capacity he traveled to France, was a companion of David Hume, years his senior, and met Voltaire and Benjamin Franklin. Smith became more interested in economics and the tension between a free market, *laissez faire*, and mercantilism, drawing a distinction between productive and nonproductive labor, a distinction between agriculture and manufacturing versus the employment and consumption of the nobility and the church, the so-called *bourgeois.* That same distinction might be seen today in the employment and consumption of the so-called 1%.

In 1766, Smith's tour as a tutor ended and he returned to Scotland, spending the next ten years writing *The Wealth of Nations,* wherein he advocated a division of labor between nations, and argued the theory that rational self-interest and competition created a self-regulating economy, an invisible hand that would guide the economy to prosperity. The theory included free trade between nations, wherein each nation's resources and skills could be optimized for the mutual benefit of each. One nation's production might favor agriculture, another silk or textiles, and yet another gray-iron and manufacturing. *The Wealth of Nations* was researched, detailed, and written in such extraordinary depth as to remove all doubt. One tends, however, to remember only the invisible hand of enlightened self-interest and interpret it as justifying greed.

The Wealth of Nations, published in 1776, the year of the American Revolution, impacted the world with a view whose timing and power were profound. Thus ended an era of mercantilism, dominated by nobility and church. However, the industrial revolution which followed replaced the nobility and the church with an oligarchy and an exploitation of labor, crueler than the agrarian serfdom that came before.

Indeed, industrial productivity created great wealth and economic mobility for a new plutocracy, along with greater and more open competition. This new economic framework, called classical economics, favored division of production and division of labor over accumulation of gold and silver, but brought with it an exploitation of labor, and a poverty that grew in proportion to the growth in wealth. Smith was a moralist; he would not have condoned the extent of poverty. Smith addressed these issues but in difficult terms—perhaps his was an assumption of a pervading moral ethic that would contain the excesses. His caution was there, however, if you pause to read it. For instance, in the first three sentences from *Wealth of Nations* Smith writes:

> *The annual labor of every nation is the fund which originally supplies it with all the necessities and conveniences of life which it annually consumes, and which consists always either in the immediate produce of that labor, or in what is purchased with that produce from other nations. According therefore as this produce, or what is purchased with it, bears a greater or smaller proportion to the number of those who are to consume it, the nation will be better or worse supplied with all the necessities and conveniences for which it has occasion. But this proportion must in every nation be regulated by two different circumstances: first, by the skill, dexterity, and judgment with which its labor is generally applied; and secondly, by the proportion between the number of those who are employed in useful labor, and those who are not so employed.*

If you read only the first two sentences and do not read the third, you miss the essence of Smith's caution and concern, a concern re-echoed in his third edition and in his other book, *The Theory of Moral Sentiments*, 1759, last edition 1790. These later works came during the period of the Scotch enlightenment, focusing on the morality of free trade ("The Real Adam Smith, Morality and Markets" video[22]).

Unfortunately, Smith's economics, broadly misapplied as classical economics, and the Industrial Revolution, did not lead to a sustainable égalité but became the seed of revolution. Smith, in his last edition, rejected unbalanced free trade and expanded on its problems in his later book, *The*

Theory of Moral Sentiments in 1790. Meanwhile in America, the revolution, unlimited land, natural resources, and expansion prospered with this new formula of free-for-all business and competition. Even today, with the failure of Russia's communist model, Adam Smith paradoxically reemerges in the US as the gold standard for the classical model of laissez-faire capitalism.[23]

Those who view Adam Smith's *The Wealth of Nations* as a magic bullet for free trade and unrestricted capitalism and prosperity should read the 5th edition (1790) and his final edition of *The Theory of Moral Sentiments (1790)*, published in the year of his death.[24]

Thomas Paine (1737 – 1809) immigrated to the colonies in 1774. Thomas Paine's compelling writing and his pamphlet *Common Sense* (1776) inspired the American Revolution and the colonists' demand for independence from Great Britain. *Common Sense* was so influential that John Adams said, "Without the pen of Thomas Paine and *Common Sense*, we might well have lost. The sword of Washington would have been raised in vain." Paine's *The American Crisis* (1776–83) further articulates the colonists' rejection of the English monarchy, its colonialism, its parliament, and its restriction of trade and taxation. Thomas Paine instilled the American spirit, the demand for freedom and equality. One could not fully appreciate the US economy without reading what amounts to the spirit of both the American and French Revolutions and the argument for a republic. *The Age of Reason* and Paine's later books, including *Agrarian Justice,* contributed to the framework of the American economy. He was the first to propose a minimum wage with an early understanding of the need for equality and *égalité*.

Arnold Toynbee (1852 – 1883) was the son of a prominent Saville Row physician. An articulate, attractive personality and persona, he assisted his father, as did most sons of physicians. Arnold had the best of public schools and tutoring; however, his father died when he was 18. Arnold, also in ill health, spent a year in a coastal village alone, reading and resting. The chronic illness that plagued Toynbee's short life and led to his early death came with exacerbations and remissions, a story and circumstance suggesting TB, which he may have contracted helping others on the East Side in London, or for that matter, from his father. Arnold found interest at first in the military, later dropping out of an academy, shifting interest to philosophical history. Obtaining a scholarship in modern history at Balliol College Oxford, the same school Adam Smith attended, he soon became a leader among his tight-knit group of peers, once again shifting interest to historical economics and an analysis of the poverty which accompanied the industrial revolution. Despite poor health, which prevented a full schedule, Toynbee graduated in four years, and with his speaking skills obtained a lecturing position for East Indian students. The lecturing skill soon extended to historical economics at Balliol College.

Young Arnold argued the historical method, applying direct observation of the historical outcomes, providing evidence that the so-called economic laws put forth by Adam Smith were in fact theories, relative to the circumstances, place, and time. Toynbee further argued that "Despite commonly held belief, free trade was not usually beneficial but only under certain circumstances," and that the government should regulate to a varying degree, depending on the circumstances. Young Toynbee in his lectures insisted that *The Wealth of Nations* and the steam engine had destroyed the old world and built a new one with the industrial revolution, a fixation with wealth, and a rise in poverty.

Toynbee introduced the term *industrial revolution* to the English language and studied the consequences of its explosive growth. Additionally, Toynbee rejected the concept that competition and self-interest were universally good for economic and social progress; he called it social Darwinism.

Laissez-faire capitalism had succeeded in wrestling control and wealth from the bourgeoisie only to create another problem with the distribution of wealth and proliferation of poverty. Young Toynbee argued that since the beginning of man, human civilization had attempted to soften the harsh and violent struggle for survival with a spirit of cooperation.

Arguably, economic competition is the driving force of technological and economic progress, but that competition needs to be limited to the playing field and not the general population in its universal application, like a football game with rules and a referee.

Young Toynbee died young at age thirty; he did not publish, but his students and colleagues published his lectures in the following year, *Lectures on the Industrial Revolution of Eighteenth Century England with popular addresses and notes.*

Soon after, a mission was erected in his name on the East Side in London, which stands today. Arnold's final days were spent arguing and lecturing against the logic in Henry George's book *Progress and Poverty*: he exhausted himself to that end and succumbed to his disease. Toynbee's empathy lived on, however, with the faculty and his students at Balliol College, to influence his nephew Arnold Joseph Toynbee, born 6 years later.

Henry George (1839 – 1897) born in Philadelphia of a middle-class family, dropped out of the Episcopalian Academy at age 14, and by age 15, he put to sea before the mast for Melbourne (thus missing the Civil War). Returning to San Francisco near the end of the war, Henry worked as a typesetter and with unusual writing talent worked his way up to journalist, and by 1867 editor of *The San Francisco Times*, eventually managing his own newspaper. Henry married Anne Fox in 1861. It was "a good marriage" with an Irish Catholic girl; however, against her family's wishes. Although they were poor at first, their first son, Henry junior, became a US representative for New York.

Henry's book, *Progress and Poverty* (1879) was so well written that it sold over three million copies in America and in Europe. Henry had written it while climbing a mountain near the coast:

I asked a passing teamster, for want of something better to say, what land was worth there. He pointed to some cows so far off that they looked like mice, and said, "I don't know, but there is a man over there who will sell some land for a thousand dollars an acre." Like a flash, it came over me that there was the reason of advancing poverty with advancing wealth. With growing population, land grows in value, and the men working it must pay more for the privilege.

Henry advocated a tax on the land as a tax on the concentration of unearned wealth, as a means of putting accumulated wealth back in circulation, favoring a single tax, a land tax rather than taxing labor or production. Henry supported Adam Smith and the continuation of the so-called classical economics. Land with its rapid appreciation yielded the greater return on investment for the new class of super rich. Henry George thought so doing would alleviate the poverty of the laborer without diminishing the prosperity of untaxed free competition.

Arnold Joseph Toynbee (1889 – 1975) was the nephew of Young Arnold, by Young Arnold's brother Henry, born 6 years after Young Arnold's death. Arnold Joseph Toynbee is survived today by his granddaughter, Polly, a prominent journalist for *The Guardian*. Joseph took much from his uncle's lectures and colleagues still prominent at Balliol College Oxford where he attended from 1907 to 1911. Arnold J. was a philosopher of history as well as a student of the history of economics; he later studied in Greece at the British School in Athens. Professor Toynbee returned as a fellow in ancient history at Balliol.

In 1915, Toynbee signed with British Intelligence and was a delegate to the peace conference after the war. Later, Arnold became a professor at the

University of London, and at one time a correspondent for the *Manchester Guardian*; later yet, a professor at the London School of Economics. Unlike his uncle, who lectured and did not write, Arnold J. wrote copious volumes, but was much influenced by his predecessor.

Arnold Joseph published great volumes on history, culture, and economics. A true philosopher, Arnold studied 26 civilizations, documenting their rise and fall, each realizing its unique potential and then collapsing because of some inherent flaw. *A Study of History*, in 10 volumes, was published in 1934 and again in1961. Toynbee was on the cover of *Time* in 1947; he held enormous influence in foreign affairs. Toynbee was one of the most widely published academics of all time. Other works include *Civilization on Trial, The Prospects for Western Civilization, The Economy of the Western Hemisphere* and *Why Nations Fail: The Origins of Power, Prosperity, and Poverty*. He also wrote, *Lectures on the Industrial Revolution,* basically a rewrite of his uncle's lectures. One cannot take a critical view of the present economy without reading some or all of Toynbee: the history of the same things happening again and again.

Plato (424-348 BC) was a philosopher in classical Greece and the founder of the Academy in Athens, the first institution of higher learning in the Western world; he was the student of Socrates and the teacher of Aristotle, and along with Hippocrates, the founders of Western science, inductive reasoning, and logic—much of which we have lost sight of today.

Looking back, one can see a reflection of our own struggle, both political and economic, in the writing of Plato, *The Republic*, especially chapter (or book) VIII, where he outlines the problems with democracy, oligarchy, and economics. Plato philosophically defines four forms of government: tyranny, oligarchy, democracy, and a compassionate prince; he discusses at length the way democracy deteriorates into oligarchy when senators learn how to manipulate government in such a way as to advance their own power and wealth.

Thomas Piketty (7 May 1971) While a liberal in his views, Piketty remains a solid historical economist with historical documentation going back over five hundred years. Piketty in his book, *Capital,* documents the way invested capital grows faster than income, thus accounting for the intransigency of our elite resulting in maldistribution of wealth and capital divergence. Piketty is currently proposing a tax on personal capital throughout Europe.

Born in a Paris suburb to parents who were a product of the 1968 protests, Piketty entered École Normale Supérieure on a science track at age 18, studying economics and math. Piketty earned his PhD on the subject of wealth redistribution at the London School of Economics at age 22. He taught economics at MIT from 1993 to 1995; in 2000 he became professor at EHESS school for advanced studies in Paris. He published his seminal work, *Capital in the Twenty-First Century* (2014), based on fifteen years of research directed to understanding the dynamics of wealth and income based on data covering three centuries and more than twenty countries. In 2006 Piketty helped establish the Paris School of Economics, where he is the department head.

Piketty's book, *Capital* (2014) captures the mechanisms by which wealth accumulates in the hands of a privileged few at the expense of a fair share of discretionary income for everybody else, and why that loss of liquidity for the rest of us leads to, or correlates with, recessions, depressions, wars, and revolutions. Piketty supports the correlation between recession and accumulated capital through extensive historical graphical comparisons further illustrating the mechanism through simple equations.[25]

With these fundamentals derived from historical context, Piketty goes on to show the many mechanisms favoring the accumulation of wealth within the 1%, fundamentally illustrating the economy of capitalism and a disequilibrium favoring the accumulation of capital.

Piketty suggests taxing capital more than income and urges this to be done on an international level with international cooperation rejecting nationalistic solutions:

> *When the rate of return on capital exceeds the rate of growth of output and income, as it did in the nineteenth century and seems quite likely to do again in the twenty-first, capitalism automatically generates arbitrary and unsustainable inequities that radically undermine the meritocratic values on which democratic societies are based. There are nevertheless ways democracy can regain control over capitalism and ensure that the general interest takes precedence over private interests, while preserving economic openness and avoiding protectionist and nationalist reactions.*

Political Economists

Capitalism is the astounding belief that the most wickedest of men will do the most wickedest of things for the greater good of everyone.

—*JOHN MAYNARD KEYNES*

John Maynard Keynes (1883 – 1946): Keynesian economics viewed short-term and depression cycles as driven more by demand than by productive capacity. Thus, Keynesian economics came to be known as demand-side economics. Prior to Keynes's arrival on the stage, and for Keynes prior to the depression, classic economics, especially in America, held that customer demand/need would most always exceed the capacity to produce, and if a surplus did accrue, the price would drop to the point of assuring consumption. Keynes later came to believe that surplus production would result in layoffs and thus decrease consumption.

Keynes was born in Sussex, England. His father was an economist and administrator at Kings College, Cambridge, and according to Britannica, his mother was one of the first graduates from Cambridge. Maynard entered Cambridge in 1902 with a scholarship and an interest in math and the classics; his BA came in 1905 and with a shift to political economics, an MA in 1909. After graduation, Keynes took a position with the India Office at Whitehall, resulting in his first book on Indian currency in 1913. Returning to Cambridge, Keynes lectured until 1915 when he moved on to England's Treasury. In 1921 a Russian ballerina captured his heart with a romance that led to marriage in 1925. The marriage, though childless, was lasting despite Keynes's bisexual tendencies.

Keynes' major work, *The General Theory of Employment, Interest, and Money* (1936), argued against austerity, favoring government spending. Keynes suffered ill health, including multiple heart attacks after World War II, and died in 1946 at 62.

One of the great mistakes is to judge policies and programs by their intentions rather than their results.

—MILTON FRIEDMAN

Milton Friedman (1912 – 2006) was born in Brooklyn to young immigrant parents from eastern Europe, Jeno and Sára, who struggled with a dry-goods store. Friedman finished high school and earned a scholarship to Rutgers, graduating in 1932, and an MA in 1933 from the University of Chicago, where he met Rose Director, a fellow student in the economics department with whom he had two children. Later earning a PhD from Columbia in 1946, Friedman taught and did research in Chicago. In 1976, Friedman received the Nobel Prize in Economic Sciences for his "contributions to consumption analysis and to monetary history and theory . . ."

Friedman challenged Keynesian economic policy beginning in the 1950s, favoring privatization, deregulation, and lower taxation, promoting an alternative macroeconomic viewpoint known as "monetarism." Friedman argued that a steady, small expansion of the money supply was the better policy; his ideas influenced government policies, especially during the 1980s; it became known as the Chicago school of economics. Friedman's monetary theory even influenced the Federal Reserve's response to the global financial crisis of 2007–08.

In some ways Friedman was libertarian; he favored eliminating the draft, free market, floating exchange rates, and abolishing medical license, as well as legalizing drugs with a free market. One position most difficult to support was Friedman's argument favoring privatized medical care—health care is not a free market and the current failure of that assumption could not be more obvious. On a more egalitarian level, Friedman favored a negative income tax for the poor, school vouchers, and free choice of schools. Friedman was an economic advisor to Ronald Reagan, the supply-side economist, and probably the most influential economist of the latter half of the 20th century.

Friedman's works include: The theory of Consumption Function (1957), Capitalism and Freedom (1960), Studies in the Quantity Theory of Money (1956), and Monetary History of the United States (1963).

The tension between Keynesian economics and Friedman's classical economics echoes the tension between the wealth of capitalism and the oft resulting poverty and, to some extent, the political conflict of today. Friedman espoused a supply-side economy while Keynes argues a demand side—the chicken-or-the-egg question of which came first, "eggenomics or chickenomics." The argument renders both sides irrelevant in that you

52

cannot have one without the other as well as "chicken feed," liquidity. Economists overlook the simplest of their own concepts of supply and demand. You can't have one without the other and ample liquidity on the demand side. When all the liquidity accumulates on the supply side, game over. Like Monopoly, 4 hotels on Boardwalk and everyone else is out of money: game over. Think supply-side market liquidity!

Joseph E. Stiglitz (1943) Professor, Columbia University, School of Business and Department of Economics. He is co-chair of Economic Performance at the Organization for Economic Co-operation and Development (OECD). In 2001 Stiglitz received the Nobel Prize in economics, markets, and information, and again shared a Nobel Prize for climate change in 2007. Stiglitz was born in Gary, Indiana. He received his PhD in 1967 from MIT. Stiglitz was chief economist and senior vice president of the World Bank (1997–2000); he was also a member of the President's Council of Economic Advisers from 1993 to '95, and received many other accolades.

His books include *Making Globalization Work* (2006), *Globalization and Its Discontents* (2003) with a revision in 2017. Stiglitz writes prolifically and has published numerous other works on world macroeconomics.

Significantly here, Stiglitz appears to be one of the few contemporary economists writing objectively—although with political bias—about globalization and its shortcomings.

* * *

Supply-side economists take a more classical—by that they mean laissez-faire—view, basing their interpretations on the supply side of the free enterprise supply-and-demand system. The theory holds that lower taxes, less regulation on business, and greater privatization would lead to job creation, lower-cost products for consumers, and because of the lower taxation, a greater discretionary income for consumer spending. Advocates further argue that, along with decreased government spending, the resulting increase in economic activity would increase taxable income sufficiently to make up for the lower taxation rate, thus resulting in adequate government revenue overall. Unquestionably, capitalism, with our venture capital system, capital markets, and the resulting reward for innovation, creates unmatched economic growth, expansion and jobs.

Keynesian economics, on the other hand, dominated in the recovery period following the Great Depression and in the post-World War II period of growth. Keynesian economics claimed that free enterprise alone leads to excessive cycles of growth and stagnation and that the Federal Reserve and government could stabilize the economy through policy, interest rates, regulation, and government spending in the public sector. Essentially, a consumer side macroeconomic theory, Keynesian theory stressed a more socialistic solution, reflecting a lingering fear of the Great Depression. The tax rate was high on upper income. The economy boomed after World War II. Inflation helped pay down the war debt. Tariffs were in place as well. Keynesian economics lost favor with the high interest rate and stagnation of the '70s. The struggle with communism and later the all too apparent failure of the Russian economy, proved that a centrally regulated economy was doomed to failure.

As for modern monetary theory (MMT), currently discussed among politicians—in brief, it suggests printing money outside of the International Monetary Fund (IMF), unaccounted for, like the Bank of China. An appealing means of pouring money into much-needed infrastructure and into the demand side of the market, but it runs the risk of over-indebtedness, inflation, and a monetary shotgun marriage with China wherein we are the pregnant bride.

Then too, there remains the propensity for the left to address human resources on the basis of human need and political persuasion, while the businessman would prioritize the human factors on the basis of marginal return and diminishing returns along with political accommodation.

Talking one theory or another still begs the question, though: Which comes first, the chicken or the egg? It's the human element, however, that drives productivity—at least until we replace people with robots—and it is people who drive demand. If people are hurting, you get less productivity and less supply-side market demand. It comes down to velocity, productivity, and a healthy population in the broadest sense. That energy you feel on the street, that multiplying effect closely correlates with productivity and liquidity both individual and collective. Economists at a fundamental level struggle with this concept of velocity, while it's common sense to small business and people on the street.

It seems clear that short-term business cycles result from the credit/lending cycle of over-leveraging followed by paying down debt. These swings are ongoing and relatively easy to follow and predict. The longer-term depression, some say recession, is harder to predict and understand. Piketty shows this long-term cycle to be more dependent on the concentration of wealth, thus loss of liquidity in the consumer market.

Neither of the two views of economic cycles account for the impact of deficit- globalization, when factories move to China or Mexico, when companies outsource labor and support services, and a mass migration invades our country illegally, while encouraged to do so, for cheap labor and other political considerations: a new dimension in our economy. The question emerges: To what extent can we afford to handicap our own citizens in favor of unbalanced international trade?

Today's capital divergence finds 40% of US wealth, 98 trillion, living with the top 1% of households, variously reported. Added stock market liquidity from credit easing has done little for productivity. Credit easing, however, did lead to overpricing of the equities market where increased capital chased a finite number of equities. The risk remains from stagnation on the demand side of the consumer market and from the enormous debt incurred by the process of credit easing. We likely still run the risk of a major depression or a cataclysmic redistribution,[26] a redistribution by revolution, war, famine, or plague. Russia or the CCP might promote all four.

CHAPTER 8. OLIGARCHY

When democracy which is thirsting for freedom has evil cup bearers presiding over the feast, and has drunk too deeply of the strong wine of freedom, then, unless her rulers are very amenable and give a plentiful drought, she calls them to account and punishes them, and says that they are cursed oligarchs.

—*PLATO'S* REPUBLIC *BOOK VIII*

The accumulated capital and sequestration of wealth within the top 0.1% and a growing oligarchy stifles the economy, leading again and again to depression or war. Government accountants, the Fed, the accounting office, and political economists, not to mention legislators, fail to identify the long-term cycles of depression and the capital divergence characterized by accumulated wealth sequestered in the equities and bond market, hedge funds, shadow banking, dark pools, and offshore tax havens.

Best evidence suggests US internal investments amount to $3.673728 trillion,[27] while offshore financial centers hide another estimated 3 trillion[28] in US dollars. The US share of capital hidden in international tax havens was less than European dollars and by another lower estimate of approximately 1 to 2%, of a total of 21 to 32 trillion international tax-sheltered dollars and growing.[29]

Specifically, our economists fail to acknowledge the obvious, that outsourcing manufacturing, service, jobs, and revenue to foreign countries—to the benefit of our own multinationals and international banking interests—has had a deleterious effect on the American people. Indeed, globalization levels the standard of living between the US and developing countries but at the expense of the US taxpayers, and to the benefit of the supply side, a process supported by a near-religious and perpetuated belief in globalization and a fantasy that unbalanced trade is the same thing as free trade—some of which is true, but with an end result of extreme exploitation of our own hard-won egalitarian culture, energy, and our standard of living. It's the consumer's discretionary income and wealth, multiplied many times by business and consumer activity, that results in prosperity. Our consumer's discretionary income and wealth lost to and multiplied by China, Japan, or Germany's business and consumer activity resulted in China's, Japan's, and/or Germany's prosperity.

Oligarchs here at home continue to exploit our consumers to the benefit of what now amounts to a class society, one that resembles the aristocracy before the American and French revolutions. Was the wealth of the oligarchs earned through free and not-so-free enterprise? Of course it was, but without a means of limiting the perpetuation of accumulated wealth, democracy fades into a society of oligarchs who feel justified in their station and have little regard for those who desire a life less driven to compete. The resulting inequality fosters a class society as harsh as that of the early Renaissance: a class society, the antithesis of the American culture of hard work and opportunity. Plato warned of democracy deteriorating into an oligarchy or tyranny. We can have one or the other but not both.

$$Democracy \underset{Wealth}{\longleftrightarrow} Oligarchy$$

$$S + (m\text{-}x) = I + (g\text{-}t)^{30}$$

where S = domestic savings; m = imports; x = exports; I = investments; g = government spending and t = treasury revenue

Economists, both historical and political, paint a history of the struggle to manage a society that champions both freedom, equality, and corporate enterprise. They struggle to balance the cornucopia of free enterprise with the elements of human need, and to afford security, safety, education, and health, with access to nutrition and shelter for the population at large.

Historically, the perfect storm of the American Revolution, the French Revolution, Adam Smith, and the steam engine, led to a shift away from an economy of monarchy and nobility with a dependency on mercantilism, colonialism, pillage and plunder. There emerged an industrial revolution, an industrial and merchant class, and maritime trade. Classic economics, defined as self-regulating, was a shift from the aristocracy to the manufacturing and merchant class, from bourgeois to laissez faire, as the Adam Smith wrote, "but with great prosperity came great poverty." Additionally, industrialization led to the same capital divergence we see today. The accumulation of wealth in the hands of a few leads to a depression, thus the term *boom and bust* cycle that has characterized capitalism ever since.

To be complete, history needs to mention Karl Marx. Most of western philosophy disputed Marx's criticism of capitalism because he had no viable plan to replace it, save tyranny, or oligarchy, but certainly not democracy. Additionally, persistent Marxist philosophy throughout the Cold War and even now, ensures an overreaction favoring unfettered, unregulated capitalism, citing the collapse of the Russian Federation as proof of the failure of communism and the superiority of free enterprise. The Chinese CCP, furthermore, has been successful in spreading its own communistic capitalism along with pillage and plunder and with its newfound wealth, creating oligarchs out of thin air—and an ancient kind of bribery.

Capitalism is the champion of the West, but like a runaway bull, it creates great productivity and wealth and is the bedfellow of democracy, but like a bull it needs control lest it suck up all the consumer (market-side) oxygen and stomp up all the grass. Controlling the downside of capitalism without crippling it remains the unmet challenge since the Industrial Revolution. Without a way to prevent a few players winning all the script or a way of redistributing the wealth, rather than game over and depression, as with a game of Monopoly, we condemn ourselves to an endless, long-term cycle of prosperity, boom and bust.

With globalization, we had written with a poison pen, and it included all the problems of the past with all the new twists enumerated above. Now with the CCP embracing globalization as their expansionist road map, the problems grow. The biggest of these might well be the loss of our democracy to a new kind of international oligarchy if not a surrender to a Chinese 5G dystopia.

CHAPTER 9. HUMAN CAPITAL

Globalization took a disproportional tole on the productive 90% of the US population. Job loss, plant closings, stagnant growth, and foreclosures soon led to poverty, malnutrition, lack of shelter, depression, poor health, poor morale, and suicide. These were the human factors of production lost to a generation. If labor represents the critical second factor of production—land, labor, capital, and entrepreneurial ability, it also constitutes the major share of the consumer market. The deterioration of human capital was as great as the loss of income and liquid capital.

As a society, we voluntarily created an economic structure within which we could function cooperatively. Globalization failed us with a burden that we did not volunteer for. Business at any level looks to its human resource as critical to long-term success. Both the employer and government share responsibility for the human factor. Without a healthy, secure, well-housed, well-fed workforce with high morale, productivity lags, and what's worse, the market lags as well. Both the intellectually elite and laissez-faire marketers, the government, too, loses sight of this fundamental cause for market stagnation. Business at any level tries to support the human factor; most companies of any size have a human resource department in support of their employees. Successful businesses promote a culture of caring, efficiency, and high morale. Those considerations should drive the political balancing act between the free hand of multinational corporations and basic humanity, liberty versus égalité.

Thomas Paine in his book, *Agrarian Justice,* makes the point that in the natural state, that is, without the structure of government, banking, property ownership, and so forth, each individual processes a natural and equal claim to the land (1.7 acres of it if we divide habitable land by world population), and the ocean too, for that matter. Paine goes on to suggest that when private and government ownership came about, that ownership owed a debt or rent to the natural owners, which includes all of us. Paine equates the natural right with culture and society itself, a cooperative venture in which the people form a government to serve their needs, not the other way around. In the natural state, all men and women are free and equal and thus process a human capital and first deed to the earth. In his book, *Agrarian Justice*, Paine goes into detail, how improvements on the land logically belong to the current owner, but that improvement and its productivity owes rent to the living population. At length, Paine suggests a payment of 15 pounds sterling to every person on his or her 21st birthday and another 10 pounds starting on their 50th with 10 pounds a year thereafter for life. Like property tax and insurance, Paine calculated the life expectancy and rent required to balance this debt and suggested handling the debt like obligatory bonds. Thus, human capital would be funded as a natural right of the individual, not a benefit, granted reluctantly, by the government or corporation. We do indeed charge property tax at the local level and pay it back in the form of police, school, and fire protection, sometimes hospitals.

Globalization, computers, the internet, outsourcing of labor and services, outsourcing of manufacturing, and multinational corporations lead to a capital divergence (the maldistribution of wealth). This unprecedented concentration of wealth in the hands of a few, held in investment and shadowy banking, led to a sequestration of wealth, like in the 18th century Industrial Revolution, and in 2009, led to a second great recession, from which we are only now recovering.

With prosperity on the supply side came the loss of consumer liquidity, poverty, and arguably the depression. Unfortunately, the depression did not result in a redistribution of wealth. The taxpayers bailed out the investment banks. Subsequently, investment banks merged with commercial banks, insuring taxpayer protection for further overleveraged investments. The consequences of the bailout persist, not just from the excessive concentration of wealth, capital divergence, but from the poverty and the struggles of the middle class and everyone else. The list goes on: college graduates who cannot earn enough to pay their obscene college debt, 3.4 million homeless (a fourth of them veterans), some 3 million empty houses sitting idle on the balance sheets at full value in the banks that foreclosed on their fraudulent loans, seniors forced to go back to work or rent out their homes, a record number of incarcerated prisoners—many for drug-related charges or convicted for stealing food. We have the worst public health statistics of any developed nation: an unacceptable burden of disease, malnutrition, decreased longevity, infant mortality rates, and yes, starvation. Meanwhile, our leadership has attempted to export dysfunctional governance to the rest of the world as an example of democracy and capitalism. With the poverty and stagnation comes depression, obesity, despondency, misbehavior of every sort, including suicide and cultural rejection. The intellectual elite and the media with multimillion-dollar salaries remain blind to the reality, in part justifiably because the scale, in the trillions, is too large to see, and those who are well off protect the status quo, not unlike *The Hunger Games,* where media project a perception through rose-colored glasses.

The US health care system suffers from too few physicians, poor continuity of care, too high a cost, and poor outcome. That's another story, not unlike the divergence of capital. Poverty, poor nutrition, depression, obesity, a drug and opioid epidemic, displacement resulting from globalization, came at a bad time—overburdening our monopolistic, largely incorporated private sector and dysfunctional medical bureaucracy.

The maternal mortality rate in the US in 2014 was 23.8/100,000, a 26% increase from 2000. The morbidity rate increased 200% since 1993 and currently accounts for 144 complications per 10,000 deliveries.[31]

Life Expectancy[32]

Between 1959-2016 US life expectancy increased from 69.9 years to 78.9 years but declined for 3 consecutive years after 2014. The recent decrease in US life expectancy culminated a period of increasing cause-specific mortality among adults aged 25 to 64 years that began in the 1990s, ultimately producing an increase in all-cause mortality that began in 2010. During 2010-2017, midlife all-cause mortality rates increased from 328.5 deaths/100,000 to 348.2 deaths/100,000. By 2014, midlife mortality was increasing across all racial groups, caused by drug overdose, alcohol abuse, suicide, and a diverse list of organ system disease. The largest relative increases in midlife mortality rates occurred in New England (New Hampshire, 23.3%; Maine, 20.7%; Vermont, 19.9%) and the Ohio Valley (West Virginia 23.0%; Ohio, 21.6%; Indiana, 14.8%; Kentucky, 14.7%). The increase in midlife mortality during 2010-2017 was associated with an estimated 33,307 excess US deaths, 32.8% of which occurred in 4 Ohio Valley states.

The Global Burden of Disease (GBD), from the WHO[33] shows the US ranking among the 37 nations sharing statistics with the Organization for Economic Cooperation and Development (OECD). Add to the list: worsening infant mortality and longevity statistics, and you have a truly discouraging statement of US public health.[34]

Alzheimer Disease	33rd – of 37 countries
Poisoning	34
Lower Respiratory Tract Infections	23
Cardiomyopathy	31

HIV/AIDS	29
Chronic Kidney Disease	31
Colorectal Cancer	8
Breast Cancer	16
Other Cardiovascular and Circulatory	22
Hypertensive Heart Disease	27
Stroke	9
Kidney Cancers	31
Pancreatic Cancer	23rd
Leukemia	2nd

Figure 2. US Burden of Disease ranking among 37 of the developed countries participating in the Organization for Economic Cooperation and Development (OECD)

Among the findings for 2018:[35]

- When combined, cases of syphilis, gonorrhea, and chlamydia hit an all-time high.

- More than 35,000 cases of primary and secondary syphilis were reported, the most since 1991. This is an increase of 14% between 2017 and 2018.

- Newborn syphilis cases exceeded 1,300, a 40% increase. Arizona, California, Florida, Louisiana, and Texas accounted for 70% of the cases. Deaths from congenital syphilis increased 22%.

- Over 580,000 cases of gonorrhea were reported; again, the highest count since 1991.

- Chlamydia cases rose 3% to over 1.7 million, an all-time high.

The health care sector offers jobs with good pay and security, but the burden on the low end of the economy further reduces discretionary spending, and as such, paradoxically adds a further loss of consumer liquidity, a further anchor and stagnation to the economy.

Intriguingly, globalization might have been a benefit to our health care system. Free movement of physicians, drugs, patients, insurance, hospitals, and capital could have solved many problems. Historically, the best physicians were those who sought additional knowledge in foreign medical schools.[36] But, despite all evidence to the contrary, we still insist on the superiority of US medicine. With respect to some advanced techniques, the US does lead, but not in overall outcome. The very proponents of free trade legislate against patients purchasing their prescriptions from countries where drug prices are not overblown, part of a misguided compromise awarding monopolistic advantage to the pharmaceutical, hospital, and insurance industries.

For longevity and life expectancy, the US comes in 42nd. These numbers should be a major embarrassment for our claim to a superior form of government and economy. We cannot expect to have a churning, vibrant economy, or a worthy quality of life with this level of ill health. The economy, most of all, reflects the health of its people.

Food insecurity: Semistarvation haunts 30 or more states including 13.1 million children, according to Feeding America and the USDA. That's in addition to 5 million seniors over 60; it goes hand in hand with poverty. How can we spend trillions on the new world order, globalization, and military misadventures while neglecting our own vulnerable people struggling through no fault of their own? Interestingly, World Life

66

Expectancy Rates reports that the US is now 119th out of 172 countries in malnutrition, ahead of Azerbaijan and Bulgaria. What more can be said? The United States won't be productive until we shore up these human factors, provide security, the rule of law, plug the liquidity drain, and replace the lost wealth of the American people.

Unemployment, displacement, and high cost of housing drive homelessness and depression. The estimates of homelessness run more to than 3.4 million. Of these, 12% are veterans, 67% families, 74% children, 25% mental, 17% chronic, 33% single parent with children, and 13% fleeing violence. Since 2006, banks foreclosed on 17 million homes, with 24 million filings, and 5 million repossessions, figures greater than in the Depression of the '30s. Among seniors, 10 million face hunger, 20 million over 50 go without adequate finances, and 19 million over 50 cannot afford their housing costs, with options severely limited.[26]

The 2015 census estimated over 6 percent of the homeless live in motorhomes, RVs, vans and cars. The Council on Economic Advisers in America, September 2019, estimates over half a million homeless, 65% in homeless shelters and 35% outside shelters on the street or in cars. The National Alliance to End Homelessness confirms these figures with a total of 567,715, 395,000 individuals, 172,000 families, 96,000 chronic, 37,000 veterans, and 35,000 unaccompanied youth. One needs only to count the foggy windows in a Walmart parking lot at midnight to get an idea. Local government's only solution has been to ban all sleeping-in-vehicles in public places, which has done little more than turn the problem into an "out of sight out of mind" situation, pushing people onto the streets of cities and into unsafe areas with drugs, crime, and less access to job opportunities. The numbers of people (visible) living curbside in recreational vehicles are said to have decreased since 2017; however, the numbers of people living in cars or on the streets in "tent cities" in major cities such as Los Angeles, San Francisco, Chicago, and other places have been steadily increasing. Clearly,

America still faces a massive challenge, but at least it now acknowledges the problems.

* * *

First Russia, and now China, wage a cultural and economic war against the US, sowing hate and chaos wherever they can. In 2019, 23,000 kg fentanyl from China was intercepted by the Marina-Armada, at a southern Mexican port, bound for the US[37]. The shipment originated in Shanghai and was bound for Culiacan, Sinaloa, home of the Mexican drug cartel. Fentanyl[38] is not only a major health threat to our people, but a direct result of unemployment. The CCP's attitude, if not sponsorship, of the formulation and export of fentanyl to the US constitutes an act of war. The fentanyl homeless occupy the sidewalks of Seattle and LA. We desperately need state-of-the-art psych hospitals for drug detox, recovery, out-of-control children, major psychiatric disorders, and the care of those who just can't cut it. Addressing these issues would, furthermore, move us toward identifying the tragically emerging psychopathy associated with gun violence. Unfortunately, "progressive" psychiatric thinking in 1961 addressed the problem of poorly managed psychiatric hospitals by closing all of them. Legislators voted with the attitude that mentally ill patients could find care in their local communities. These were issues of freedom versus safety, tax savings, and the convenience of psychiatrists at the expense of local communities.

CHAPTER 10. EDUCATION

One has to rewrite history in order to justify reliving it with the same disastrous results.

—THE AUTHOR

Globalization necessitated perception management in our schools in order to mold the attitudes of our youth; it has done so, but at what cost? Next to basic security, there is nothing more critical than education. We grew up in this country letting children out of school early to help with farming and the harvest. It is clear that less than a high school diploma leaves the dropout disastrously vulnerable. Less than college education closes the door to most well-paying jobs. It seems equally clear that living on the street after 16, when school is no longer mandatory, leads directly to violence, drug abuse, and civil disorder, as currently seen in Chicago, Baltimore, and elsewhere. We supply lots of liberty but little equality with this minimal requirement and provision for education.

The Program for International Student Assessment (PISA) ranks US students—while 3rd in innovation and 1st in female science students—35th in math, 29th in science, 18th in reading, 28th in preschool students (3yo+), 14th in college graduation, 24th in high school literacy and 134th for government commitment to education.

Given reasonable security and health, education carries the greatest weight in promoting citizenship, responsibility, and a work ethic, thus productivity. Obviously, rapid advances in technology, robotics, and artificial intelligence demand a higher level of technical education and training.

Student loans threaten another crisis, not unlike the subprime mortgage crisis, with a probability of a similar outcome. Privatization, a successful strategy in competitive markets, fails in health care and remains questionable with education, largely due to limited choice and monopolistic pricing. School choice may help. Market pricing works when the buyer is free to walk away and has viable alternative choices, a case that rarely exists with illness or with education. That's why both qualify as critical infrastructures. By promoting college loans to minors under the age of 21, to borrow unlimited funds to pay unlimited and growing college tuition, legislators did what they do best—shuck responsibility and cost onto the most vulnerable, those without a choice, in this case minors, thus rendering them indentured to the banking industry for most of their lives. In 2008 Congress passed legislation making bankruptcy relief from student loan debt illegal under bankruptcy laws; they did the same for mortgages before the mortgage crisis of 2008. The student debt now exceeds 1.4 trillion USD with over half of students in debt on average for over 30 thousand dollars.

Furthermore, colleges welcome wealthy foreign students—wealthy on their favorable balance of trade with the US—who are more than willing to pay high tuition costs. Additionally, supply and demand push tuition costs even higher, crowding out US students with greater financial need and less favorable academic records. This is globalization at its best, but unfortunately, best for the other guy—just one more burden on the working class.

Politicization of our education system may be the worst of the education reforms in our schools. History was once a story of how we got here and what happened along the way. The student riots of the anti-Vietnam era and later the perception management from the CFR as well as the TC, and diversity-driven student activism began a process of revising curriculum requirements for graduation, ultimately eliminating large swaths of history from study. Both Russian and Chinese NGOs further the ideological subversion and corrupt the education of vulnerable American youth. The goal of racial equality seems hijacked by politics, foreign NGOs and a clash of unassimilated cultures. A celebration of diversity and entitlement replaced or discouraged the study of history and western civilization. Heather McDonnell, in an interview about her book, *Diversity Delusion,* remarked, "I think without sounding apocalyptic or extreme, I think we are playing with fire. We are putting civil peace at jeopardy because it is impossible to overstate the degree to which students are being taught to hate, not just Western civilization but each other." Many would call McDonnell's caution an overreaction. However, we see her worst fears played out on the street, and evidence of Russia's long-standing ideological subversion and now massive infiltration and bribery from the Chinese People's Republic (CPR). At the very least, education deserves a civil debate and a major overhaul, and freedom from foreign interference.

CHAPTER 11. POPULATION

He only says, "Good fences make good neighbors."
Spring is the mischief in me, and I wonder
If I could put a notion in his head:
Why do they make good neighbors? Isn't it
Where there are cows? But here there are no cows.
Before I built a wall, I'd ask to know
What I was walling in or walling out,
And to whom I was like to give offense.
Something there is that doesn't love a wall,
That wants it down.

—ROBERT FROST, *1874-1963 MENDING WALL*

In 1798, Thomas R. Malthus wrote *Essays on Population*, correlating depression and poverty with the rapid growth in population and with concern for the food supply and health. Today's world population estimate of 7.7 billion, and growing by 82 million per year, already challenges our resources, reminiscent of Malthus's industrial revolution. Some 80% of the world population lives in poverty on less than $10 per day.

America's not-so-civil debate on immigration did not consider the issue of mass migration. To date, the US has seen only a foreshadowing of mass migrations. America no longer had unlimited farmland for the welcomed masses but rather a significant probability of importing poverty and disease, further depressing the already challenged infrastructure. Legal immigration remained a plus, but mass migration promised disaster. Even legal immigrants send money "home," amounting to an added drain on the demand-side liquidity.

In the early days, immigration drove the expansion of the West; it provided the labor, entrepreneurial ability, developed the land, and drove productivity. Population growth adds to the economy up to a point, a point of diminishing return. Immigration had grown the American economy and still does. However, overpopulation erodes stability, safety, the environment, and civilization itself, as demonstrated throughout history.

The utopian view of globalization would maintain open borders, where workers can go wherever work is needed and pay is good. It works in Europe and even stopped Europe's endless wars; however, today's influx of refugees threatens stability and safety. Refugees today may be only the tip of the iceberg.

Will offering asylum to refugees fleeing tyranny do anything to oppose the tyranny? If capable people flee, who remains? What happens when a country loses the majority of its skilled laborers? Where then will a country acquire the resources for those remaining? If such a situation becomes more widespread, might failed states not constitute an additional threat? A benevolent monarch, or prince—to use Plato's words—may be the only form of government capable of controlling the chaos and anarchy in some of these cultures. Nation building with artificial democracy has not worked. In the words of Thomas Paine, freedom and equality are there but only for those who want it.

According to the Earth Institute, 10% of the world's population lives in coastal areas in crowded conditions. Coastal flooding, as recently seen in New Orleans at the time of hurricane Katrina, promises further migrations.

Another imbalance involves oxygen and carbon dioxide. Never mind global warming, there is a limit to the CO_2 concentration we can breathe, beyond which CO2 becomes toxic. The toxic effects already affect our oceans, and we all know we need oxygen. The simple answer is more trees and fewer people.

Jeffery Sachs, author of *Common Wealth* and *The End of Poverty*, outlines these challenges of poverty and overpopulation with convincing quantitative research but with an optimistic—utopian—outlook. Sachs's optimism requires great global cooperation, which as one can observe, leaves much to the imagination. Jeffery writes, "Sub-Saharan Africa's population has more than quadrupled, from 180 million to around 820 million" and there's more to come by way of economic convergence and better health care. Sachs predicts Asia becoming the dominant economy with the power and population in China and India (a trumpet sound of surrender). "The forecast deemed to be the most likely, envisions that the global population will rise from 6.6 billion in 2007 to 9.2 billion in 2050."

The total habitable surface area of the earth amounts to 15.77 billion acres; that's down to 1.7 acres per person, still good enough for a victory garden but not much more, and we still need the trees and enough greenery to reduce CO2 and generate O2. Per forest management, the cycle of respiration requires 22 trees per person[39], so a victory garden must be well shaded, vegetables only. Then again, a matter of distribution.

Migration, immigration, and refugees seeking asylum will only accelerate. Given the history of natural disaster, war, famine, pestilence, and plague, mass migrations may become yet another peril of the 21st century, a massive game of musical chairs.

Sadly, there remains an issue of cultural incompatibility. John Kerry, in his rationale for the US abstaining from a vote in the Security Council resolution condemning Israel for continued occupation and construction on the West Bank, said that a one-nation solution was undesirable for (either) of the parties, that Israel could be a Jewish state or a democracy but not both.

This acknowledgement from even the most liberal and idealistic politician, paints a reality that we are slow to grasp.

CHAPTER 12. NATIONAL SECURITY

The free trade of globalism first threatened US security with a reduction of US petroleum production and independence in favor of cheap imported oil, mostly from the Middle East. National security, since before World War II, demanded a strategic petroleum reserve for emergency military demand. In 2017, deregulations and shift to an energy-independent policy eliminated the strategic vulnerability. As of September 2019, we have 645 million barrels of crude stored deep in underground caverns in salt domes along the Gulf Coast. US petroleum production had been in serious decline, partly because of environmental concerns but mainly because of the cheap oil from the Middle East. US production of hydrocarbons, now restored, still demands a balance between environmental and security issues. The transition to alternative energy for the military relies on technology and the adaptation of cleaner nuclear energy, but we effectively ended the security threat posed by globalization to America's basic energy needs and generated a significant boost to our jobs and our economy. Then too, renewable energy sources now generate more energy in the US than coal.[40]

Additionally, the offshoring of manufacturing and technology created an unacceptable security vulnerability. Corporations sought less regulation, cheap labor, lower taxes, and expanded markets. Any major conflict, however, would leave the US dependent on others for our own security. Americans excel in our freedom of imagination and innovation. How do we secure this national treasure? Intellectual property rights protect our creations, and our laws hold up in the Western world, but less so or not at all in the East and especially not in China. Utility patents last 20 years, a design patent 14 years. A trade secret lasts as long as it is commercially valuable. Trademarks last as long as they are used. Copyright protection, since 1978, lasts 70 years from the death of the author. The Digital Millennium Copyright Act (DMCA) of 1998 (for good or bad) along with the World Intellectual Property Organization's Copyright Treaty, covers the internet and extends copyright for films and music. Protection of military secrets becomes increasingly difficult with our global connectedness. In the 1960s, Paul Baran, an electrical engineer working at Rand Corporation, charged with solving the security needs of military command and control against nuclear threats, proposed a mesh network that would survive widespread disruption both from attack and from natural disasters.[41] The threat then was physical. But today, hacking from within our now global network poses the greatest security threat. Proposals include blockchain encryption, quantum computing, and data teleportation, an interesting future.

Risks of conflict persist despite profitable trade, and the list is long: China, North Korea, Russia, Iran, jihadists of various denominations, probably in that order. Globalism offered China an opportunity for war by other means. It's not our trade war. It's a trade war already won by the CCP. China had been running a serious multifaceted war against the US and the West for twenty years. A book printed in China by the PLA publishing house, *Unrestricted Warfare42* outlines in depth this multifaceted war, and serves as a road map to China's undeclared war against the US and the West. *The Art of War* by Sun Tzu,[43] an ancient Chinese philosophy of conflict, outlines the same kind of subversive conflict.

Present tariffs and negotiations appear to be the first effective response to the CCP's economic and cyber warfare. The outcome is anything but assured. We have been struggling with China's militarism for a long time. Both China and Russia fought with North Korea and that war is not yet resolved. Today's tariffs amount to the first serious response to the CCP's economic aggression. To their credit, both of our primary political parties now acknowledge the CCP threat—at least those not already compromised by the PLA's subtle and not so subtle bribery and recruitment. China now provides nearly all our generic drugs. Impurities are suspect. Nothing could better illustrate this vulnerability than the COVID 19 pandemic and our struggle to secure foreign supply chains for critical supplies. Furthermore, China exports fentanyl to the US as a means of sowing chaos. China exports overproduction and dumping to achieve dominance on nearly all forms of manufacturing. Companies that China cannot put out of business by undercutting prices, they invite to build factories in China under favorable terms. Seeking profit, cheap labor, land, less regulation, and access to China's 1.6-billion-person market, US companies have flocked to China. However, these Western companies doing business in China have also been forced to comply with technology transfer, and accept the outright theft of the company's critical technology, as well as a monetary policy not allowing the company to move money out of China.[44]

China owns and manages the port facilities in the US on both coasts. China pursues dominance over logistics and world supply chain with much success. The CCP thus controls not only the supply of vital products but also the delivery—no small security risk for the US.

Vanessa related at some length her experience with the import of coffee bags from China. The bag-manufacturing plant was massive, equipped with the most current and automated machinery. The plant offered exceptionally low prices and excellent customer service. Problems arose, however, with the Chinese national agents operating as US customs brokers in San Francisco. The shipping cost for the packages of coffee bags and the bags themselves was low, but the customs broker demanded a fee greater than the cost of the product. There was no recourse.

Meanwhile, Russia remains a threat, utilizing classic methods of spying, hacking, ideological subversion, and a further wish to repatriate bordering countries in Eastern Europe. No surprise; however, there was once a promise of bringing Russia closer to the West. The prospect of Russia's adherence to international (Western) trade and security measures supersedes the question of whether Russia embraces communism or democracy or remains an oligarchy. Russia remains an open question. The consequences of Russia's Cold War tactics against the US remain quite evident in the extreme Marxist rhetoric from the far left. Rioting, looting, vandalism, and burning lay evidence. Did Russia, China, or international oligarchs underwrite the West's summer of violence and hate?

Yuri Bezmenov, aka Thomas Schuman, a KGB education subversion specialist who defected to Canada in 1970, assumed an alias and released a book in 1984.

As I mentioned before, exposure to true information does not matter anymore. A person who was demoralized is unable to assess true information. The facts tell nothing to him. Even if I shower him with information, with authentic proof, with documents, with pictures; even if I take him by force to the Soviet Union and show him [a] concentration camp, he will refuse to believe it, until he [receives] a kick in his fan-bottom. When a military boot crashes his balls, then he will understand. But not before that. That's the [tragedy] of the situation of demoralization.

Once demoralization is completed, the second stage of ideological brainwashing is "destabilization." During this two-to-five-year period, what matters is the targeting of essential structural elements of a nation: economy, foreign relations, and defense systems. Basically, the subverter (Russia and now China) would look to destabilize every one of those areas in the United States, considerably weakening it.

The third stage would be "crisis." It would take only up to six weeks to send a country into crisis. The crisis would bring a violent change of power, structure, and economy and will be followed by the last stage, "normalization." That's when your country is basically taken over, living under a new ideology and reality.

Bezmenov, Yuri (1984). "Soviet Subversion of the Free-World Press: A Conversation with Yuri Bezmenov" (YouTube) (Interview). Interviewed by G. Edward Griffin. Westlake Village, CA. Retrieved 2020-07-08

Today it's China. Our freedom, democracy, and political system, messy as it is, work after a fashion. The more disciplined CCP, however, uses our openness and political system against us, including spying, hacking, stealing industrial secrets, and a subtle form of camouflaged bribery. This recruitment falls just short of actionable, or so compromises the recipient as to render him or her a virtual foreign agent. We have a long history of coping with Russian espionage; however, today Chinese espionage[45] matches and far exceeds the long history of Russian spying. Espionage and subversion are a major part of the PLA, employing thousands utilizing Database, AI, and 5G. The typical approach to recruiting US citizens involves LinkedIn, the social network, looking for high-level political, defense, intelligence, or scientific assets. By way of the internet, Chinese agents contact targets of interest on the internet by the thousands with flattery and interest. Recruiters make some offer of recognition along with financial support with a thin veil of masking: as if from a Chinese university, think tank, or corporation. The recruiter may offer a large stipend for a lecture, a seminar, or a position on the board of directors, plus transportation and accommodations in China. Once engaged, they've got you. The internet makes recruitment, contacts and overtures from CCP controllers far less risky than conventional espionage. Controllers sitting in Beijing can send out thousands of proposed offers on the Internet, doing so in complete safety.

The Defense Personnel and Security Research Center (PERSEREC) was founded in 1986 after John Walker, a navy cryptographic radioman, and eleven spies were arrested. The DOD organization under General Richard

Stilwell focused on trust betrayal and espionage. The executive summary[46] of a 2017 report lists a changing profile of espionage since 1990, but with only [?] 209 cases: (1) classic espionage; (2) leaks; (3) acting as an agent of a foreign government; (4) violations of export control laws; and (5) economic espionage. The report goes on to say: Motivations have changed recently, recruiting targets manifest divided loyalties, disgruntlement, and are subject to ingratiation and a desire for recognition. Recruits are mostly male, racially diverse, half are married, more educated than in the past, ¾ civil servants, ¼ military, 60% volunteers, 40% recruited. Previously spies were mostly Russian. Now agents come from China, southeast Asia, and the Middle East.[47] The above appears a paltry beginning to a massive counter-espionage challenge.

Our borders may be the toughest issue of all. Everything changed with 9/11/2001 when 19 Al Qaeda jihadists crashed the World Trade Center. Freedom of air travel was already compromised by hijackings and airport security. How do we balance security with freedom? At one level, 9/11 was a security failure, at another level, a clash of cultures and an act of war. Lady Liberty had always filtered the "huddled masses" for disease and criminality. We probably need to do the same with a closer watch for spies, smugglers, traffickers, and jihadists.

Prior to the emergence of neoconservative thinking, the new world order, and nation building, foreign policy by one ingenious statesman or another pursued a stable international balance of power. China, more exactly the CCP with two thousand years of Chinese tradition, strategizes globalization as a balance in their favor.

The Korean War was West against China, North Korea, and Russia. China eases the sanctions against North Korea, as in a game of chess, more likely a game of Go. North Korea now serves as the sacrificial junkyard dog of the CCP. This old axis between Russia, North Korea, and China remains intact. But Russia has an 11-mile border with North Korea at Khasan along the Tumen River. The Sino-Russian border, additionally, runs for 2,615 miles to the west separated by the Ussuri, Amur, and Ergun Rivers. Russia, with a population under 147 million, 77% west of the Urals, an area of 6.6 million square miles, much of it forest land and agriculturally fertile, is largely unprotected. China may be covetous with food shortages and a dense population of over 1.4 billion living on 3.7 million square miles. Russia may be inherently vulnerable to Chinese globalization. Russian expansionist goals in eastern Europe must be contained but moving Russia away from its close ties with both North Korea and China seems prudent, a balance of powers. Hold your enemy close.

PART 3
RESOLUTION & CRISIS

CHAPTER 13. CONFRONTATION

After each country found out how easy it was to tax itself rich by way of tariffs, each country taxed itself rich the same way. Then the cities and towns of each state taxed themselves rich by the same way, and finally Mother taxed herself rich by putting a whopping duty on the roasting ears Pa brought home to cook, then Pa voted himself a two hundred per cent duty on the fur coat he bought for Ma's birthday, and ... "G'wan, that's too silly for anything." "Oh no! It's the economic philosophy of the two historic parties that govern this great and intelligent nation."

—OSCAR AMERINGER

Professor John Ise had found little redeeming about tariffs,[48] citing the advantages of trade, the irrationality of protectionism, the common false concept of market, the benefit to only a few, the injustice, the burden on farmers, industry, wages, employment, concentration of wealth and so forth. Ise dismissed tariffs as a tax and holds that exports must equal imports in the long run.

However, Ise acknowledged the infant industry argument, wherein protection for industrial growth across the board could allow new industries to grow to the point of international competitiveness, a time when the protection could end. He gave the example under Alexander Hamilton in the early nineteenth century, of spectacular American industrial growth. Ise went on to write, "If the entire world were on a secure basis of commercial amity, peace, and goodwill, international dependence would involve no serious dangers; but . . ." And he went on to recognize a strategic military desire for self-sufficiency. Furthermore, he wrote that the diversification of industries protected against the violent ups and downs of business cycles versus an economy based on a few product lines—all of these exceptions characterized the deteriorating position of US manufacturing in 2016. Ise suggested a balance between the dangers of foreign reliance and the cost of trying to maintain self-reliance. The balance between self-reliance on oil and the potential cost to the environment can serve as an example, comparing the cost of self-sufficiency versus the cost of strategic vulnerability. The US chose the former. Professor Ise further recognized the necessity of retaliation. This leads us to the present situation and a retaliation against a 20-year war by other means, an economic war, waged by China's CCP against the Western world.

The present use of tariffs as a weapon of negotiation constitutes a special case. Furthermore, the economic environment is not at all free trade, but a highly distorted aberration due mainly to the CCP, the emergence of multinationals, and outsourcing. Anti-tariff theories advanced by politicians, multinationals, investment banks, and the media—some out of ignorance but most out of self-interest—cloud reality. "Tariffs are a tax paid by the customer." No, in this unique environment, tariffs on Chinese goods are paid by the importer to the benefit of the Treasury Department's revenue or offset by the exporter or the foreign government. "Everything will cost more." No, not for long, if at all. Goods will soon be more affordable relative to increasing consumer employment and liquidity. "We started a trade war." No, we lost the 20-year trade war started by China. Globalists cost us our middle class, our wealth, and our dignity. It will take years to earn back our wealth but earn it back we will. "The economy will crash." No, the economy will grow due to the multiplying effect of added consumer activity multiplied by the added employment and liquidity. "It is dangerous to grow

85

our GDP faster than 3%." No, rapid growth benefits us all, and we need to catch up. (Historically, the bursting of the so-called "bubble"[49] was engineered by our FCC-sanctioned phone companies, to extend their monopolies and control of the internet.[50]) "There will be more unemployment." No, as is already true, many more jobs and companies will return to the US.

Those who will actually hurt are Wall Street banks and multinationals as they are forced to give up the cheap labor and investment activity financed by lost consumer wealth. They, too, will adapt, and US laws will once more encourage fair behavior and customer service.

Tariffs before World War II correlated with economic growth. Since then, growth rather correlated with a more liberal trade.[51] Many economists struggle to understand why. Might it be that since World War II, the US subsidized international trade? Starting with the Marshall Plan, US taxpayers financed the recovery of Germany, Japan, South Korea, and Vietnam and now China. We continued to do so under globalization.

NAFTA and the proposed Pacific Trade Agreement were unbalanced in a similar way.

The economics of globalization looked much different from the street than from Washington.

Favored trade agreements had been a major part of the spectacular postwar recovery. We naively extended the same policies to China, hoping they would embrace the Western system of law and rules-based mutual trade. China did not embrace Western values, but rather initiated a militaristic, expansionistic, and predatory economic war. We now have a 25% tariff on Chinese imports. We'll see what happens. A trade agreement that does not include the rule of law and reasonably balanced trade, benefits only multinationals, banks, politicians, and the other guy—at the continuing expense of the US taxpayer.

What actually happens with the payment of tariffs? The Chinese product arrives at a US Customs and Border Protection warehouse in the US. The US customs broker pays the tariff at the customs house on behalf of the importer before the product can be released from the customs warehouse. The money then goes directly to the US Treasury. The importer may look to another country for the product or to a US supplier. The Chinese exporter can reduce the selling price, or the Chinese government can subsidize the manufacturer or devaluate the yuan to offset the cost of the tariff. The customer can make an alternative purchase; it's called elasticity of demand. With any significant price increase, the customer will walk away or go elsewhere. China can retaliate by not buying imports from the US or impose the same stiff tariff on us. But since Chinese imports from the US amount to far less than US imports from China, the leverage is not there for China. China can retaliate by dumping US treasury bonds, which they have done before, and by devaluating their currency (already dropped from .15 to .14), or blocking the export of rare earth metals, a strategic product. There are risks, more to some segments of our market than to others. Our current policy of tariffs, if reciprocated, may hold risk, especially for our farmers.

If the US customer chooses to buy an alternative product made in the US, that choice will impact our economy significantly in a positive way, while affecting the Chinese economy in a negative way. The consumer's discretionary dollars would no longer leave the country but would remain in US markets. With multiple turnovers, the liquidity left in the US market economy will have a multiplying effect on the GDP. Furthermore, that positive addition to the GDP, and that added liquidity, would accrue to the consumer's side of the market, not to the supply side, thus rebuilding some of the lost wealth of the American middle class. US businesses planned for these tariffs and will adapt. The US will be stronger for dealing China out and confronting their predatory trade practices. The rest of the world will benefit as well. This is a contrarian and timely view of economic reality based

87

on liquidity and actual numbers. In the long run, tariffs may depress the economy as most economists insist. Ise wrote, optimistically, that in the long run exports will of necessity equal imports. I'm not so sure. Our biggest challenge is to pull together and not defeat ourselves from within. Buy American!

Macro Economics, Wayne Godley, T Francis Cripps, 1983

$$S + (m-x) = I + (g-t)$$

Increased revenue to the Treasury raises t, on the right, necessitating either more government spending, g, investments, I, or decreased imports, m; thus, adding liquidity to the demand side. (Speculative, but some support from the year-end numbers. We'll see what happens.)

Another way to look at it:

$$(I - S) + (G - T) + (X - M) = 0$$

Problematic? Were tariffs inflationary? Probably. The merchant having paid the tariff by way of his or her customs broker faces a choice of increasing prices but can only do so rationally within the limits of his or her own price and income formula—*elasticity of demand*. A percentage increase in price results in a certain, perhaps known percentage loss of sales. The customer is free to choose an alternative purchase as well. Minimum wage was probably inflationary too. There is no doubt that the grocery shopper pays more than a few years ago; hopefully, with more local products and fewer Chinese chickens. Inflation as reported by the BEA was 1.4%in 2018; 1.6% in 2019, so yes, they were probably both inflationary as artificial perturbations of free-market movement. However, the percentage price increase remains significantly lower than the reported increase in both income and spending (see chapter 14). Arguably, the inflationary effects of tariffs and minimum wage were small compared to the liquidity and wealth they drive from the supply side of the market back to the demand side, to the people. Inflation is not bad if you have a lot of debt, including the national debt. On the other hand, if you live on a fixed income, inflation hurts. The Fed would like to see 2% inflation. *Others would prefer to see silver dollars.*

CHAPTER 14. POST GLOBALIZATION

The voice of rebellion chills the air. As Americans remain divided, China wages unrestricted warfare[52] against America without firing a single shot. We obsess, not just with the traditional duel between left and right, or between liberty and equality[53], but rage on over:

- Globalism versus nationalism. Globalists passionately argue for the return to a failed internationalism that led to an economic and security disaster here at home—capital from our once wealthy, now decimated, middle class, and the American taxpayer-financed foreign policy giveaway.

- Much of corporate America turning a blind and greedy eye to our own people in order to gain access to China's market of 3.6 billion people.

- Wall Street bankers continuing the use of American workers' own pension funds to "invest" in unregulated Chinese companies.

- The WTO billion-dollar loans to China, again underwritten by the American taxpayer.[54]

- Our own Silicon Valley resisting all attempts to limit outsourcing of jobs, chips, and manufacturing.

- Washington bureaucracy, under much foreign influence, resisting any change in policy contrary to their own (and China's) perception of a new world order.[55]

- Both Congress and courts attempting to override or negate executive action, a constitutional issue.

- Military, industry, and State Department urging our armed forces to police the world at a devastating cost to our taxpayers. Young soldiers are placed in harm's way (Neocons and the US's New World Order).

- Politicians, while unconcerned about Russia's alliance with North Korea and China, raging against any constructive engagement with Russia.[56]

While we fight among ourselves, blind to anything but our own self-interest, China goes on a shopping spree, buying up South Pacific islands, especially those with strategic naval significance, all with *our own money*. Wake up, America, and pull together.[57]

* * *

Globalism ended abruptly in 2017 when a populist backlash surfaced in the US, reversing many of the unintentional destructive elements of internationalism: outsourced manufacturing, jobs, mass migrations, and national security. The subsequent economic recovery remains both dramatic and contentious. The presidential election of 2016 led to an abrupt rejection of an intransigent bureaucracy clinging to internationalism and the New World Order. The shift left unresolved issues and massive resistance to the change. What went well and what did not?

Growth in manufacturing and productivity

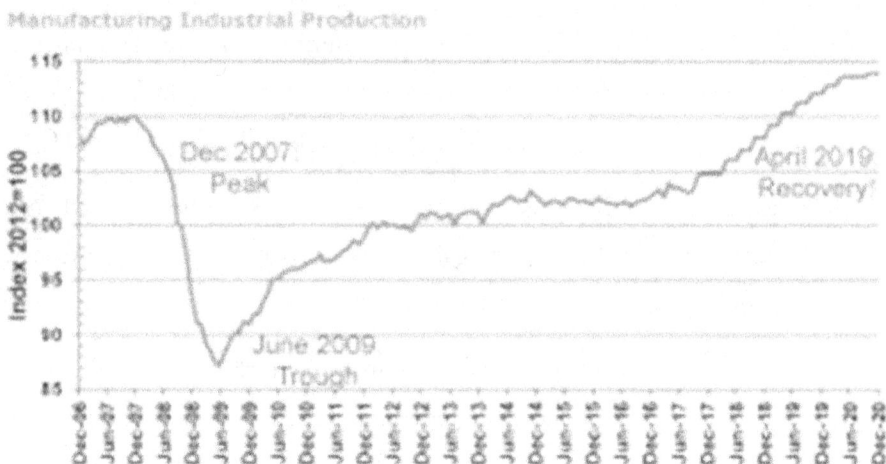

Manufacturing Industrial Production

Index 2012=100

Dec 2007
Peak

June 2009
Trough

April 2019
Recovery'

Sources: Federal Reserve Board and MAPI Foundation

Then the Chinese Corona virus struck. If anything, the pandemic further illustrated the extent to which US loss of manufacturing even the most rudimentary personal protective items and basic pharmaceuticals, along with the loss of control over the supply chain, rendered the US vulnerable and insecure.

Globalism as a vicious predator, devouring our demand side wealth, lies wounded but not dead. Labor reemerged with increased wages and decreased unemployment. Small business returned with increased manufacturing. The Treasury balance, national debt, grew by almost 6%, just over half of the budget shortfall last year, but a staggering 23.2T. Personal savings with nominal personal investing grew a surprising 8% year over. The trade deficit shrank by 14 %. All good news except the national debt, but whether our strategy continues to succeed, or whether sufficient to regain our lost national treasures of manufacturing and citizens' wealth remains a question. Furthermore, the internationalists, the multinationalists, and the minions from the dark side, the CCP, and miscellaneous oligarchs, will certainly try to resuscitate the wounded beast, and return to globalization's deficit paradigm based on supply side gain and demand side plunder.

The GDP divided by the M1 leads to an estimate of the turnover or velocity in the economy, a fundamental economic concept not often followed. The estimates of GDP and M1 at the end of the 4th quarter 2019, 21.429 and 3.9231 = 5.46, a significant increase over 2018, but far less than the 10.9 high of 2007.

DTR 20200206	2018	%	2019	Δ [i]
National Debt	21.917T	7.10%	23.210T	+5.9%[52]
Nominal GDP[ii]	20.580T	2.90%	21.429T	2.30%
Treasury Revenue 20200206	1.037T		1.095,193T	5.6%[iii]_[iv]
Annual Rep. BEA Jan 31, 2020				
Personal Income	17,819.2B	5.60%	18,624.2B	4.50%
Disposable Income	15,741.5B	6.10%	16,438.0B	3%
Personal Consumption	13,998.7B	5.20%	14,563.9B	4%
Personal Savings	1,210.4B	7.70%	1,311.5B	8%
Price Index (inflation)		1.40%		1.60%
Corporate Profit, 3rd Q				-0.20%
Trade Balance	-627.679B		-550.123B	14.10%
Customs/Tariffs 20190206	28.654B		33.574B	17.20%

$$S + (m\text{-}x) = I + (g\text{-}t)$$

$$(t\text{-}g) + (S\text{-}I) + (m\text{-}x) = 0^{58}$$

Increased tariff + increased savings + decreased imports = zero

Government + private + foreign = zero[59]

These numbers suggest that the average consumers experienced a 4.5% increase in income, a 3% increase in disposable income, bought 4% more stuff, and managed to save 8% more than they did a year ago. As of October 2019, unemployment fell to 3.5%, the lowest level in 50 years. Inflation, however, plays an ugly role, but according to the yearend BEA report, only a 1.6% increase compared with 2018. That includes lower fuel costs and higher grocery costs distorting the picture, depending on one's petroleum consumption. Corporations did not do as well. Although these numbers can be spun, and they often are, it's hard to argue with their implications and consistency. The 8% increase in savings did come as a surprise, suggesting some consumers paid off debt. The point may be contentious, but suggests that the supply side, including importers and China, absorbed most of the tariff. The demand side of the market should benefit from increased discretionary income, increased market liquidity, and the apparent increase, though small, in market velocity (turnover). The gain for small business and the working population, for now, makes up for the pain felt by large corporations and multinationals. Again, a flow of liquidity from the supply side to the consumer side of the market returns a fraction of the wealth lost to globalism, big business, and bad deals with a few foreign entities. Employment opportunities, wages, discretionary income, and consumer spending are up (see above). Manufacturing growth and corporate profit are slower than consumer spending and tend to confirm the much-needed reversal of globalism's liquidity drain from the demand side of the market. This is a speculative explanation for what the numbers indicate. The equation is nonintuitive, but a close look supports a change for the better, with a liquidity flow to the left. Might these numbers not reflect the early recovery of our economy resulting from the re-negotiated trade, MCA and Japan, the minimum wage and opportunity zones, along with an insistence on fair trade with China, while both inflation and the national debt remain concerns? Furthermore, free trade ideally remains the ultimate goal but only between compatible and trusted trading partners under viable rules-based trading.

These optimistic numbers do not account for the lower end of the scale. Despite improved employment, poverty, homelessness, mental illness, and addiction plague the streets of many cities. Furthermore, manufacturers who continue to depend on exports to China may need to make hard decisions whether to seek other markets. Manufacturers with plants in China might reconsider, as might US fabless corporations, whether or not to continue manufacturing in or outsourcing work to China.

The flow of illegal immigrants appears to have slowed (but with an estimate of 14.3 million illegal immigrants in the US). The cost to US taxpayers may reach $131.9 billion.)[60] Work off the grid and transfer of income back home create a significant further liquidity drain. This is not a political argument. There is no question that legal immigration built this country and will continue to do so. However, an uncontrolled, unvetted flow of migrants runs contrary to our history and our laws, whether crossing the desert or arriving on United. In the past, immigration policy considered the need for assimilation. Today a more destabilizing view favors the opposite.

Our forebears spent their time on Ellis Island, 1915. We vetted arrivals for infectious disease and much more carefully than we do today, and today's immigrants pose the same public health problem.

We appear to be avoiding further nation building and police actions with slow withdrawal from those in progress. An end to the New World

Order and military engagements could be good or bad; we will see what happens. Some would call the disengagement a transition from military warfare to economic warfare. We now appear to recognize the size of both our economic loss and the extent of the economic and cyber war the CCP has directed against America since China's admission to the WTO in 2001. Furthermore, we began to recognize the extent of US capital market investment in China and the number of these securities, and vulnerabilities, held by US institutions and retirement funds.[61] It also turns out that most of China's high-tech giants, now competing with our own, were financed by our own stock exchange, but without the listing documentation and auditing requirements demanded of US corporations.[62]

Contrary to conventional wisdom, tariffs reemerge as a major driver of US market liquidity and consumer wealth, as it has in the past.[63] Though a useful tool in restoring fair and balanced trade, free trade among trusted partners still remains the ultimate goal.

Although we have experienced substantial economic recovery, we still have a long way to go in restoring the lost middle-class wealth, the manufacturing might and technology leadership that characterizes US free enterprise. That leadership together with consumer wealth and confidence builds our economy.

Remaining vulnerabilities:

- The optimistic numbers do not account for the lower end of the scale. Despite improved employment, poverty, homelessness, mental illness, and addiction plague the streets of many cities.

- CCP globalization is war by other means.

- We remain vulnerable to cyber warfare.

- Corporations continue to manufacture in China; China's population on Jan 2020 was 1.409,136,010 billion[64], with a GDP of 12.24 trillion in USD.

- Our recovery, strong as it is, may take decades to replenish all that was lost.

- Loss of political ethics, courtesy, and cooperation has caused extreme polarization.

- Bureaucratic and legislative establishment undermine executive strategy.

- Disregard for citizenship, democracy, and the rule of law is widespread.

- Media and education system continue to be politicized.

- Health care is in decline, opioid epidemic.

- Student debt is in crisis: 4.7 million loans, $1.6 trillion.

- Democracy is moving toward oligarchy.

- Maldistribution of wealth continues: "capital divergence."

China, the CCP, continues to use our own freedoms against America and the western world. They encourage manufacturers to build plants in China to gain strategic technology, make loans that cannot be repaid, and prevent profits from leaving the country.

An example of the CCP's capitalistic communism and globalization, China-style, includes the lucrative harvesting of organs from prisoners and minorities scheduled for reeducation or termination. Xinjiang province is home to most of the country's Uighur. The US State Department estimated in early 2019 that up to three million[65] Uighurs might be imprisoned for "free vocational and reeducation training"—or elimination. Prisoners receive

CAT scans and DNA histocompatibility studies upon admission and serve as a reservoir for à la carte organ transplants. Satellite views show crematoriums adjacent to these reeducation camps and hospitals. Sound familiar? Only Israel forbids its citizens from going to China for an organ transplant. There is no waiting list, no waiting time, x matched organs on demand.

CHAPTER 15. PANDEMIC

COVID 19 came as a shot out of the blue, whether from a wet market or the accidental release of a deadly virus from a level-4 laboratory, the CCP suppressed the knowledge and permitted travel from Wuhan, releasing a fast-spreading virus, to the rest of the world. China denied any person-to-person spread of the virus. The WHO investigating the outbreak confirmed the CCP's claim. The WHO's press release January 12, "Based on preliminary information from the Chinese investigation team, no evidence of significant human-to-human transmission and no health care worker infections have been reported." WHO tweeted the same statement on January 14. When the WHO first acknowledged person-to-person transmission on January 22, the US had already identified an Illinois woman on January 21, who had traveled from China a week earlier, and developed pneumonia with COVID 19. Her husband became ill a week later and tested positive for the virus.

The CDC issued warnings January 6 to 8 and started screening passengers from Wuhan on January 16. President Trump created a pandemic task force January 29 and blocked foreign travel from China on January 31; he was called racist by his opponents for doing so. By February 18, COVID 19 had spread throughout China and 26 additional countries.

The stock market crashed February 24.

Amid controversy, POTUS pumped sunshine in an attempt to mitigate the fear and help stabilize the market amidst uncharted territory, fear of the pandemic, and concern for possible banking and business failures.

By February 26, CDC confirmed community spread. By February 29, the U.S. experienced a severe shortage of PCR test kits and personal protection masks, face shields, protective uniforms, ventilators, and respirators. Nearly all such supplies came from China and China was no longer delivering. Plus, the demand soon overwhelmed all prior stocks of medical supplies and equipment and most alternative supply chains. Many US manufacturers dropped everything and shifted manufacturing to meet the production need for testing, ICU equipment, and supplies. Time needed for both production and delivery, however, caused further problems for health care workers. On March 13 the US declared a national emergency, thus giving the government power to demand help from companies and protect against profiteering. Companies, however, needed no persuasion and came to the rescue in a manner that can only be described as heroic (Ford, Honeywell and others). All this is history.

As of August 18, 22 million cases have been reported worldwide, 783 thousand deaths, 3.5%. In the US, the Corona virus accounted for 176,321 deaths by August 22, with a death rate of as high as 6.06 in May, which may have been due to underdiagnosis, falling to 3.11 by August, presumably with better diagnosis and treatment. By the end of September, the death rate per reported case fell below 3%.

By August 26 there had been 5.8 million cases. New deaths per day peaked again April 16 to 19, averaging 4.6 thousand. The low during the first recovery April 6 totaled under 200 deaths per day. Then the second resurgent peak around August 6 averaged about 1.6 thousand deaths per day. As of late August, the US death rate had fallen just below a thousand deaths per day. The stock market made new highs, ahead of an expected further economic future, which remains in doubt.

Epidemic	Perspective Mortality	Penetrance	Yearly Deaths
Smallpox	30%	high % of pop.	
Bubonic Plague	50-70%	high % of pop.	
Pneumonic Plague	100%	Increased virulence	
1918 Flu	27%	809 / 100,000	675,000/2 yr.
TB	26%	46 / 100,000	
COVID 19	3.11%	53 / 100,000	199,421/8 mo
2017-2018 Influenza	<0.1%	7.3 / 100,000	79,400
Ebola	11 cases treated in US		4
Heart Disease			647,457
Cancer			599,108
Chronic Lung Disease			160,201
Stroke			140,383

If the same measures applied in Africa by the CDC and WHO for Ebola, had been applied in China with the first outbreak, control might have been possible. COVID 19 spreads aggressively, like chickenpox or influenza, by way of surfaces and aerosolized droplets.

This pandemic all but destroyed the prior economic recovery. Faced with conflicting choices, the US acted decisively in closing the border. Daily briefings with the two main CDC epidemiologists informed the public, encouraging best practices to mitigate the spread of the virus. The U.S. administration shut down the economy.

Amidst political controversy, the administration balanced death and destruction from a closed economy against the 3.11% death rate from COVID19, opening the economy by states. State governors have the constitutional and legal authority and responsibility for public health decisions, and US public health had always been managed state by state. The governors reopened their businesses following national guidelines.

Many young people and those less compliant ignored the guidelines, forming gatherings and parties, thus leading to the second spike in cases and deaths from the virus. The balancing act between death and suffering from the closed economy and deaths from the virus remains a political as well as a public health and national security controversy, an open question that is hard to quantify. Reopening schools proves an even greater challenge. A vaccine and more potent anti-Corona virus drugs will be critical for recovery. A possible resurgence of the epidemic in the fall challenges pharmaceutical companies to come up with vaccines and better antivirals. Four companies have vaccines in stage III trials. The federal government ordered volume production of the vaccines before final approval by the FDA, hoping for the approval, thus making possible an urgent distribution of the vaccine.

The longtime deemphasis on public health, despite our CDC and some outstanding epidemiologists, further handicapped the government's response to this epidemic. Both isolation and quarantine contradict the public's constitutional right to freedom, further compounded by the citizens' right to confidentiality. Eighty years ago, Public Health had teeth and authority to override those civil liberties of freedom and confidentiality for the quarantine and the common good. The H1N1 flu of 1918 killed 50 million and 500M cases gave Public Health respect, a respect that slowly declined. Hopefully, the US may once again build a vigorous Public Health service and a more accessible and affordable health care system.

CHAPTER 16. SUMMARY

Globalism worked well in closed systems of fair trade with regulation and the rule of law, such as between states in the United States or within the European Union. It did not work well with colonialism or early communism, and it's not working so well for us with the predatory practices of Communist China, or with the unbalanced tariffs and trade previously negotiated with others. Many trade policies subsidized the trading partner to gain friendship or to encourage a more trusted engagement. Cynically, we had been subsidizing our neighbors with the prosperity of our middle class, our taxpayers, and the consumer side of the market. US taxpayer wealth seemed an infinite resource, but time proved that it was not. Outsourcing led to increased unemployment and poverty; a 15-trillion-dollar drain on the liquidity from the buy side of our market economy from unbalanced trade alone. The ivory tower of academia missed the simple street side fundamental of liquidity, supply, and demand. China, Germany, and Japan posed the greatest problems. Trading partners retained their own tariffs or practiced other nontaxed obstructions to trade.

Globalism was nothing new except for our present internationally led, nonelected NGOs, primarily the TC and the CFR. This was something new, an internationalist consortium of unelected and unappointed elitists directing our foreign policy and trade.

The Phoenicians, Alexander the Great, the Roman Empire, and the British Empire—even Communist Russia with its own central management formed international trade structures under their own unique laws. Ostensibly, most efforts were to create mutual trade benefit. Unfortunately, and especially with colonialism, pillage and plunder lay not far beneath the surface. Most notably, Roman globalization was comfortable with conquest, slavery, and feeding Christians to the lions. The Roman Caduceus (misrepresented only in the US as an icon for American medicine) in Rome symbolized a bilateral free trade, globalism, between nation states or trading entities, the two intertwined snakes, under the protective wings of Roman law. The Chinese version of globalization sounds much the same with conquest, indentured labor, and a not-too-friendly attitude toward Christians. Fair trade and the rule of law, however, were never China's goals.

American globalization began as an ideal of promoting international cooperation, international banking interests, and the hope that free international trade would mitigate bad behavior and expansionism by less friendly powers. Globalization promised prosperity to most of the world by offering the same free trade, openness, and prosperity enjoyed by the EU and the US.

Politically, the Left embraced globalization on the basis of idealism with decreased nationalism, increased international loyalties, and a sense of spreading the wealth.[66] Conservatives on the right embraced globalization for the Adam Smith laissez-faire, magic hand of self-interest. Free trade, and the modernized concept of division of labor, further justified the outsourcing of both manufacturing and labor along with unrestricted immigration for cheap labor.[67]

Globalization driven by a shadow government with its shift to a more international ethic became so well indoctrinated in schools, the media, and the public that globalization became a moral imperative and a new standard of political correctness. Despite all evidence of the problems, globalization came to dominate US think tanks and all branches of government. Economists held steadfast to the conviction that the efficiencies of globalization would eventually benefit all concerned.

Sadly, the outcome of globalization fell far short of the expectations. The outsourcing of jobs led to massive unemployment. The displacements, unemployment, and poverty resulting from globalization's division of labor far exceeded the minor displacements that economists' models predicted. Economists reluctantly apologized for Congress not passing entitlements in support of those displaced by the outsourcing of labor.

The mass migration of refugees and illegal immigrants was not the division of labor Adam Smith had in mind. Desperate as they were, these were families and children, not migrant workers or skilled workers seeking work where their skills were most needed. Many immigrants send earnings back home in support of families remaining behind. Doing so shed a further drain on consumer-side liquidity. Living off the grid did so as well. Legal immigrants, on the other hand, compete for jobs, in Silicon Valley or the medical/ health care fields, some a corporatized immigration strategy. We import grade school teachers from Guatemala and give immigrants our graduate school slots.

Within the continental US and Canada, free movement of labor occurred within reason, driving substantial shared economic gain. Open borders worked well in the EU as well with only a humorous complaint about the amorous exploits of the Polish plumber. This open-border policy applied to international mass migrants, however, took place in defiance of US laws. Overpopulation, failed nation states, persecution, and poverty continues to drive mass migration.

We cannot blame the failure of US immigration laws, world overpopulation, and poverty, or failed nation states on globalism. We can look to the New World Order, as advanced by multiple administrations, for forcing a clash of incompatible cultures, mainly the East versus the West. If globalism was intended to prevent wars and spread democracy and personal freedom to trading partners, it appears to have done the opposite. Sadly, wars were not prevented by globalization, but rather promoted, with enormous loss of life, lifelong disability, and a staggering cost to our taxpayers.

The outsourcing of manufacturing eroded US manufacturing capacity to a service economy and back to a service and agricultural base. The loss of our energy production, steel and aluminum fabrication, as well as rare earth mining and processing, created a national security crisis. The outsourcing of computer and chip manufacturing eroded our future leadership in information technology. China's theft of intellectual property, trade secrets, forced technology transfer, and predatory trade practices took the loss to a critical level.

Cheap labor in underdeveloped countries did not lead to the expected development in those populations, but rather another form of exploitation, often brought about by local corruption and our own misadventures in nation building.

Economists failed to quantify the massive drain on liquidity from the middle class, the poor, and the consumer market, a drain of capital that found its way into trade deficits, investments, foreign assets, and into the shadowy investment banking world. Economists insisted that the trade deficit did not matter and that any displacement would have corrected itself, leading to the benefit of all concerned—eventually. Economists point to the accounting reality that trade deficits are in US dollars, and investment worldwide.

Street drugs, foreign purchases, investment in foreign corporations, sending money back home all deplete demand side liquidity. Whereas, alternative purchase of US made products, increased US manufacturing, productivity, jobs & income, grow demand side wealth at the expense of the supply side.

(Depleted Middle Class) Demand = Supply (Capital Divergence)

$(S + (m-x) = I + (g-t)$

Democracy or Globalism

(Where S = domestic savings; m = imports; x = exports; I = investments; g = government spending and t = treasury revenue).

The formula economists refer to as sectoral balance shows a balanced accounting, wherein money lost from trade deficits and consumer savings goes to investments, government spending, or treasury. The formula does not quantify whose investment, whose government, or whose treasury. If you think about it, the equation does more accurately imply a flow of liquidity from the left side of the equation to the right, a flow of money and wealth out of circulation, out of the hands of the majority of American people and into supply-side profit and sequestered assets. The capital lost in the trade deficit goes to foreign profit, foreign government, and a little of it returns as foreign direct investment in US bonds, equities, businesses, and property: assets built on the lost liquidity and wealth from the American people. When you follow the money, China and others drained vast consumer and middle-class wealth from the consumer or buy side of the market to foreign capital and capital investment. This reality, discounted by economists, was far more obvious from the street than from the ivory tower. Globalism and cheap labor further produced extraordinary profits for fabless technologies, including internet, chips, computers, and cell phones. Furthermore, the resulting abundance of investment capital financed China's astounding growth, their military, and their adoption of globalism as their new formula for CCP expansionism.

The goals of free trade and international cooperation are not dead, nor should they be. Globalization, however, cannot go on as it is: at the expense of our people, our democracy, and our rule of law. We are destroying ourselves from within. Our two-and-a-half-century experiment in democracy is not over. The outcome is not assured. We risked losing our democracy a few times before, with our Civil War, a Great Depression, Korea, Vietnam, and multiple failures in the Middle East. Our democracy now faces a new economic challenge from a new kind of market communism that embraced globalism as its own and executed an aggressive economic exploitation of the West, every bit as effective as the West's exploitation of China with the opium trade in the 1800s. Our leadership, media, and education system blinded us with a hysterical mindset for globalization at any cost, anti-nationalism at any cost, and surrender to this new wave of globalistic communism. It does not hurt that our democracy is contentious and messy, but it does matter that we actually see the numbers and stop fighting among ourselves long enough to regain lost ground and insure our future prosperity and liberty.

"Think globally and act locally," reflected the mindset of international citizenship and a denouncement of nationalism. Theresa May wisely said, "If you are a citizen of the world, you are a citizen of nowhere." International cooperation is one thing, but the current discounting of and disregard for citizenship, both in our schools and our legislature, further threaten our culture, our democracy, our constitution, our freedom, and ultimately our security. If globalization was the cause of this discounting of citizenship, we have yet another reason to study our alternatives going forward.

CHAPTER 17. FAST FORWARD

You can have democracy, or you can have globalism, but not both.

Without further documentation or evidence, we offer thoughts for debate. Predicting the economy, like predicting the stock market, affords no crystal ball, but we can ask a few questions and explore a few ideas. There needs to be an open civil dialog about the pros and cons of globalization, the China threat, education, capital divergence, public health, climate change, 5G, and political gridlock, even the meaning of citizenship.

Globalization resulted in our educating those from other countries while neglecting our own. Education, if nothing else, should be our first priority. Forget the mandate of public education up to the age of 16. That may have been adequate way back when we were an agrarian society, but today we are at the bottom of the ladder for education in the industrial world. Mandate education to the age of 18. Provide a technology-path alternative to traditional college curriculum with little or no tuition. Arrange paid internships in various career fields. The current opportunity zones show the potential benefit from a partnership between education and business. Allow multiple pathways. Include the arts, music, and more relaxed pathways for those who struggle with education and competition. A mandatory one-year military service for all, male, female, other, no exceptions, might be good. It works in Switzerland. Such an experience might facilitate the much-needed assimilation of immigrants and their cloistered divisions. Again, if nothing else, education should be our first priority, including civics, parenting, civility, and ethics. A bit of discipline wouldn't hurt.

What can be done about propaganda disguised as education and news? Perception management from China, Russia, globalists, the oligarchy, and other-directed self-interests, dominate mainstream and social media and colors our education system. We might insist on a separation of actual news from editorials and prohibit anonymous sources with FCC regulation, much like truth-in-advertising. Schools of journalism might also consider teaching logic, Aristotle's 13 fallacies of logic, logic that remains remarkably absent from most editorial reporting.[68] Furthermore, we must block the ideological subversion from communistic governments and from within.

Furthermore, America simply cannot afford globalization's outsourcing of manufacturing, jobs, or services. We cannot afford to lose our manufacturing capacity for both economic and security reasons. We cannot afford to gratuitously subsidize the developing world for corporate, personal, or political gain at the expense of our citizens. As it is, it will take years to regain the relative wealth and quality of life we enjoyed in better times.

With regards to China, the people are good: they are resourceful and hardworking. Their willingness to be regimented accompanies a strong sense of nationalism. However, we must uncouple economic aggression waged by the PLA/CCP. Tariffs and isolation appear to be working up to a point, but thus far it has not been enough. It might not be possible, but we might better negotiate a balanced, cooperative, less expansionist, more compliant agreement to a rules-based cooperation. Better cooperation than resorting to either military or isolationist solutions, but all things considered, how do we end the aggression on multiple fronts, balance the trade, and find restitution for our losses? Tariffs and a strong military presence may remain our only leverage. In the meantime, manufacturers may need to get out of China, for their own sake, if not for US security. Our prescription drugs and generics must be secured from China and formulated in the US or other safe places. Consider uncoupling capital markets with China, securing our seaports, and balancing China trade with tariffs. Negotiate or isolate. Meanwhile there remains plenty of mischief in North Korea, the PLA, and the South China Sea, even an apparent CCP threat to Russia's vast Siberian territory.

The ancient Eastern mindset of the CCP runs contrary to Western common law and values. A treaty appears not to mean the same thing in the East as in the West. Deception remains a higher order of good in the Eastern mind. Negotiation from a western value base may be doomed from the start. We will see what happens.

Capital divergence, the economists' name for the extreme concentration of wealth in the hands of fewer and fewer people, resulting in part from globalism and the liquidity drain, poses a risk of stagnation and or major recession. Piketty favors taxing personal capital, as a means of redistribution of wealth. A tax on net assets, however, invites the transfer of assets to a sheltered untaxed offshore haven. Taxing inheritance, furthermore, undermines the greatest personal motivation for achievement and productivity. Another idea involves taxing high levels of sequestered wealth at the brokerage level where a small percentage tax yields high dollar Treasury revenue, providing the dollars to improve our critical infrastructure. Redistribution by taxation, however, poses the further question of how to distribute. Minimum wage had been one alternative. Negative income tax might be another mechanism of fair distribution. Opportunity zones appear to be working famously and are worth perusing further. The emerging labor shortage, too, may signal a trend towards higher wages, and along with robotics may increase productivity. Small business and demand-side market velocity might do the same for wealth. Furthermore, the apparent shift in liquidity from the supply side to the demand side, presumably resulting from renegotiation by tariff and other means, plays a further note of optimism. In any case, we need more humor, optimism, turnover, and velocity in the market. Printing more money already probes the point of diminishing return. Inflation, too, will be a major issue going forward. Inflation eases debt burden, but at what cost to those living on fixed income? Older retirees, having exhausted their retirement nest egg, struggle with insufficient Social Security. If Social Security funds were managed and invested instead of spent in the general fund, adequate distribution might be possible. Consider doubling social security benefits for older seniors coupled to an honest cost of living scale, rather than the existing miserly increase or no increase at all as in a recent administration. Employees and employers invest heavily in Social Security; it's not an entitlement.

Globalization facilitated international banking and led to the incorporation of banks, the merger of banks, and the joining together of investment banks with commercial banks—all done to the detriment of local consumers and businesses. Doing so led to increased taxpayer liability for the inevitable bailouts. If these taxpayer bailouts were to accrue to international banks, it would create yet another drain on taxpayer liquidity. It might be prudent to separate commercial banking from investment banking. Return commercial banking to the noncorporate model of the past, and limit branch banking to the local service area. These changes could increase available credit for small business and the demand side of the market along with relationship banking and a return to the lost principle of fiduciary responsibility.

Health care suffered from the import of diseases, poor nutrition, drugs (fentanyl), a depressed population, and poverty—a direct result of outsourcing and to some extent poor health habits in the US general population. The profession suffers from political and bureaucratic controls, incorporation, administrative profit motive, poor morale among physicians, poor continuity of care, and unworkable electronic health records (EHRs). We need to restore Public Health with strong legal support. We may be seeing a start with the CDC's directives dealing with the n-Corona virus quarantines, but the need goes far beyond. Start with food and water. The population also needs to embrace a safer and healthier lifestyle. This requires adequate income, nutrition, education, and security. We should look seriously at the European models of health care (private competing with public, not the single-payer British system), including mental health, psychiatric, drug, and rehabilitation-style hospitals. Health care also suffers from corporate medicine, political interference, and greed, much like the banks. Physicians struggle today with political and bureaucratic interference, much like the profession struggled with religious interference in the dark ages. Scientific and patient-oriented medicine gave way to bureaucracy, executive salaries, corporate profit, and the not-so-magic hand of greed, while pharmaceutical companies embraced both globalization and monopoly.

The intent of the international accords on climate change, while noble, did nothing for the accumulation of trash in our oceans. Boyan Slat and his cleanup machine, *Interceptor*, did far more. Public solutions to environmental problems failed. Laws against plastic disposals fall short and the oceans suffer. The carbon tax failed as well. The Chicago Carbon Exchange closed in 2010. We need international cooperation, laws against pollution of the oceans and rivers, as well as carbon, methane, and chlorofluorocarbons (CFC) emissions. The ozone layer remains broken over New Zealand due to new HCFC by-products coming mainly from China.

On the other hand, the oxidation and reduction cycle between animal life and plant life can be replicated industrially if not by trees. Such a project, if substantial enough, could be the source for rapid economic expansion.[69] Political denial and empty promises must be replaced by high-marginal-return opportunities for the exploitation of a cheap, abundant resource. Recaptured carbon might be such a resource for exploitation. Penalties may be required, but the best solution would be a high-marginal-return transition to more efficient energy sources. The transition from a petroleum-driven to a sustainable energy source will be long and painful, but we have the technology and physics to get us there. We might avoid sudden disruption of critical energy, employment, or production while focusing on more efficient, high-margin, clean-energy generation, and distribution.

According to Victor Davis Hanson, democracy has struggled with its claim to equality versus liberty since ancient Greece. In seeking perfect equality, the Athenian democracy forfeited its freedom.[70] Today, politicians striving for equality embrace the same expansion of regulated behavior, political correctness, and forced equality, as well as redistribution of wealth. Conservatives, on the other hand, insist on liberty, freedom, and laissez-faire business, and to the contrary, accept their concentration of and preservation of wealth as a given right, arguably denying opportunity and aid to those less competitive. The pendulum swings from one extreme to the other, from dystopia to oligarchy. At the very least we need balance, a balance between liberty and equality, and a willingness to mute the swings, debate the issues, and work within the Constitution. End political gridlock and bickering in favor of civil dialog.

Our future promises 5G, artificial intelligence, and robotics. In China these technologies already combine face recognition, ubiquitous surveillance, and an infinite database to monitor and control the population. The CCP weaponized 5G to control its people and as a means of monitoring and controlling others, ourselves included, noting the massive PLA hacking of Equifax. Our adoption of 5G would likewise take control of our personal data. Expect our personal data to migrate from our smartphones to the 5G network and into an all-encompassing database. Whoever controls those data has unprecedented power over our lives: our access, behavior, attitude, and our minds. We should think long and hard about who controls these data: corporations, advertising interests, politicians, the government, or even China. Privacy will become harder to secure. The benefit will offer a great convenience and an exciting free flow of information. The downside, however, threatens an Orwellian dystopia.

Our politics and political polarization will never go away. Term limits for legislators could help, but our political democracy, messy as it is, succeeds wildly. It's a democracy we must not lose. Globalization took a toll on our democracy and our Constitution. It questions the meaning of our citizenship and disenfranchises our citizens. This has gone so far as to become both a national security, legislative, and judicial problem with a sometimes violent denial of cultural and citizenship values. To conquer a democracy, one must first disenfranchise its citizens. In an attempt to diminish nationalism in favor of internationalism, it appears that we have done just that. A serious reexamination of the meaning of citizenship needs to take place in our education system, our legislature, and our media. We cannot solve these problems without exercising our responsibility as citizens and having these conversations. The greatest threat to our democracy and freedom may come from within, and once again, from a Marxist ideology, on a chill wind blowing from the West—a new capitalistic communism under the disguise of globalization.

CHAPTER 18. SLEEPING WITH THE ENEMY, APRIL 2022

End to Postmodern Neoliberal Globalism?

Globalization or Democracy—You Can't Have Both, traces the origins and historical roots of globalism and its incompatibility with representative government. No longer a theory, we can see the results. This added chapter (4/22) documents globalism's destruction of democracy, its powerful proponents, and multiple deadly mechanisms. Follow the money. Follow the greed. Follow the subversion. And follow the war. See how globalization rapes the people much like colonialism.

On February 23, 2022, history overtook us. With Russia's invasion of Ukraine, the world changed. The conflict drove currency, commodities, and logistics into chaos. The United States lost an opportunity to establish a balance of power in Asia by further courting a Russian engagement and allegiance with the West away from China, North Korea, and Iran.

Russia's invasion of Ukraine could spell an end to the neoliberal passion for globalism. Globalization, whether American, Chinese, or Klaus Schwab's New World Order, represents a clash of civilizations and colonial exploitation, the unspoken fulminator of political and economic conflict. Globalization, despite the Russian invasion of Ukraine, however, persists as the monopoly for Big Tech, the windfall profit for investment banking, and the darling of the far left. China continues with its strategy of globalism, not for international cooperation, but for world conquest and the destruction of America.

Modern attempts to homogenize civilizations with globalization have failed rather dramatically. Or have they? Build Back Better, after the war in Ukraine—if there is an after—will be a full-court press for the elitists' new world order. Even then it will be a competition between the Chinese Communist Party (CCP) and Western technocracy, oligarchy, and banking interests. It could play out in any one or more of three ways: a resurgence of cultural and geo-ethnic nations, China's New World Order, or Neoliberal Globalism with Build Back Better.

The populism underlying a rejection of globalism smoldered for decades. During the Cold War, the Canadian diplomat Lester Pearson warned that "the most far-reaching problems arise no longer between nations within a single civilization but between civilizations (within nations) themselves." Pearson predicted the evolution of non-Western nations, not in the Western paradigm, but as an evolution of multiple civilizations insisting on their own place in history. Will emerging new alliances form along political lines, as in Communism versus Western democracies, or will cultural, religious, and geographical factors determine the boundaries between nation states?

China dominates globalism today much as she did with trade along the Silk Road with the Polos of Venice. Slavery went out of style and colonialism too, until globalism rebranded them both while applauding China's spectacular growth. Then as now, colonialism promoted international trade. The ruling aristocracy in the 17th century profited from a liquidity drain on the middle class much like the globalist elite today gain power and wealth. In China and in Asia, slavery persists, adding to the unbalanced trade with the West.

China's spectacular growth comes at the expense of the West on many interrelated fronts. We list below the emerging and deleterious concatenation of events associated with globalization, These failings conspire to replace representative government with at best an oligarchy of elitists and unelected bureaucrats favoring a vague authoritarian internationalism while discounting our Constitution and our republic. At worst we face a Marxist insurrection and autocratic socialism.

Incompatibilities between Globalization and Democracy

1. Free trade, as championed by the United States, proposed free trade among all nations, and with a generous hand. Participating countries, however, especially in Asia, did not reciprocate. They exploited the US open door as their unilateral access to exploit the vast American pocketbook.

2. Germany retained high tariffs. Japan engaged in massive overproduction of automobiles, further imposing nonfinancial trade barriers to the purchase of US-made cars. China used the opening to wage, in their own words, "unrestricted war" against the United States and the West.

3. China cheated from the minute the United States established diplomatic relations in 1969, and in the face of the United States' granting China a Most Favored Nation (MFN) status. The United States made MFN status permanent in 2021, and the cheating continued, evolving into espionage. China exploited the West, not only with excess production designed to drive out competition, but with cheaper products built with forced labor (slavery).

4. The so-called spectacular success story attributed to China was built with US gratuity, investment, subsidies, technology (much of it stolen), and the American middle class buying power of the US dollar.

5. Democracies need sound economics, productivity, and growth to achieve equality in a free and liberal economy. Most of America's industrial economy, manufacturing, and labor market was forfeited to

China in support of their growth. Germany and Japan played a smaller part in America's economic and humanitarian loss.

6. The massive capital drain on US markets destroyed the middle class, and both the demand side of the market and small business, the backbone of our economy. Without the vitality, citizenship, and common sense of a middle class, the government, especially an unelected shadow government and bureaucracy, ran amok. Technocracy, oligarchs, multinationals, and investment bankers turned authoritarian and unresponsive to the people. Without a middle class, we lost our sense of citizenship, our equality, and then our freedom, devolving into a class society of a neo feudalism like what the American Revolution fought to end.

7. The money pump, $S+(m-x) = I + (g-t)$,[1] traces the liquidity flow from the buy side of the equation on the left to the supply side on the right. As deficit trade (m-x) grows, approaching a trillion dollars a year, one sees that S (consumer savings), must shrink, or I (investments on the supply side), must blossom, along with government spending (g-t). And blossom it did. The stock market looks good, but the middle class suffers stagnation, and job loss is accentuated by fentanyl from China, depression, homelessness, and a humanitarian crisis (see Velocity and M1 in appendix below).

8. Based on the macroeconomic reality of deficit trade, the money pump led to an unimagined liquidity drain at the expense of the entire middle class and the poor, resulting in a concentration of wealth for fewer and

---

[1] *Macro Economics*, Wayne Godley, T. Francis Cripps, 1983, British economist formula for financial and sectoral balances

fewer wealthy investors at the top. Economists call the phenomenon *capital divergence*, something history associates with a slow economic cycle and depression, with war, with the collapse of democracies, and with pestilence and famine. The liquidity flow was a guillotine for everyday Americans and a windfall for China and the globalists.

9. Economists minimized these problems in fear of their jobs or their students. But then came untold wealth from the recruitment of Chinese academics, the CCP-owned enterprises, and PLA agents.

10. President Richard Nixon, ended the gold standard in August 1971, thus allowing the Federal Reserve Board (the Fed) to manipulate the currency—a necessity for maintaining the GDP and for mitigating the consequences of deficit trade. Unfortunately, quantitative easing and seeding the M1 and M2 led to unsustainable inflation. Furthermore, the Fed's quantitative easing provided liquidity to the supply side, not the business, consumer demand, and working side of the market.

11. Proponent of Chinese trade, then Secretary of State Henry Kissinger went to China in '71 followed by then President Richard Nixon who made the trip in February 1972. Hollywood actress, political activist, and communist sympathizer Jane Fonda famously went to Hanoi in July 1972 in open defiance of American tradition.

12. In July 1973 Jimmy Carter, Brzezinski, and David Rockefeller, then president of the Council on Foreign Relations (CFR), formed the Trilateral Commission (TLC). Their goal was multilateral trade and cooperation. The CFR publishes *Foreign Policy*, making US foreign policy transparent to our adversaries. The TLC and the CFR, unelected Non-Governmental Organizations (NGOs) with foreign interests, dominated the administration from Jimmy Carter 1977 until the present, excepting the Cabinet of Donald Trump 2017-2020 with such influence that this shadow government virtually ran US foreign policy.

Hence: Europe, Asia, South America, and China with many Communist sympathizers took center stage as the backbone of globalization without debate or voter say.

13. Today, the Trilateral Commission remains an unelected, semi-invisible cabal of foreign and domestic elite dictating both internal and foreign policy. In 1969 Zbigniew Brzezinski wrote, "The nation state as a fundamental unit of man's organized life has ceased to be the principal creative force. International banks and multinational corporations are acting and planning in terms that are far in advance of the political concepts of the nation state."

14. Vietnam: During and after the war, student protestors, many facing the draft, rejected American institutions, rioted, occupied campus offices, burned and destroyed property. Jane Fonda went to Hanoi. During this tumultuous time, many college students embraced Communism in rebellion against the war. This hippie generation now dominates education, politics, the media, the Washington bureaucracy, and the judiciary.

15. As its first priority, the TLC planned a reeducation of our young students, encouraging a less nationalistic and a more internationalist view. They succeeded beyond their fondest dreams, but they had help.

16. In embracing globalism, young people abandoned their parents traditional beliefs, obligations, responsibilities and their US citizenship in favor of a vague citizenship of the world.

17. The TLC (1973) was the beginning of globalization as planned, but globalism presented an unanticipated opportunity for the CCP to use it against us in a war against the West, and to use globalism for their own global expansion and colonial exploitation.

18. Oligarchs and billionaires manipulated the economy, the media, politicians, and even the courts to their advantage, further eroding consensual government by the people, pushing totalitarian control. Both Russia and the CCP furthered the strategy of subversion, manipulation, demoralization, and chaos, hoping to weaken America and destroy the Western concept of liberty and democracy.

19. A new technocracy in Silicon Valley, with more capitalization than the government, constitutes yet another unelected totalitarian force, championing globalism as a business priority to ensure cheap labor and market access to China's 1.4 billion population.

20. The Supreme Count, in 2010 in the Citizens United decision and others since, facilitated political contributions by corporations. Foreign corporations could contribute through US-owned entities and various loopholes.

21. Inflation, in part due to the pandemic, but also due to a rising socialist movement, resulted in the necessary creation of money to fulfill public obligations. Some 40 percent of our population now works for government at some level. The rest of America finances their salaries and benefits. The estimated M1 at the end of 2021 rose to 22.06 trillion, a 24 per cent precipitous increase from 17.81 trillion a year earlier.

22. Institutional investors and Wall Street committed vast sums to Chinese Initial Public Offerings (IPOs) and corporations owned by the CCP, while bypassing the Securities Exchange Commission (SEC) accounting and safety requirements. Chinese IPOs were listed, nonetheless, and a gold rush of US investments in China placed many investment and retirement funds at risk.

23. The Chinese own Hollywood. The propaganda and subversion tactics feed popular culture with endless hate, obscenities, race baiting, and violence. Humor and civility as we once knew it, no longer exist.

24. Did globalization lead to the chain of events that leaked COVID19 from a US financed Wuhan level 4 laboratory? Was the plague nature's response to capital divergence?

25. Department of Advanced Research Projects Agency (DARPA) and the National Institute of Health (NIH) financed gain-of-function research and outsourced some of the research to the level 4 lab in Wuhan, China. That bit of globalist thinking cost us dearly. I doubt that the PLA intentionally released what could be called a weaponized virus, but they could have, and that's the point. Outsourcing at any level, undermines our security, our freedom, and our republic.

26. Russian KGB for over 70 years spent 85 per cent of their espionage budget on propaganda, disinformation, demoralization, race baiting, and promotion of Marxist education in our schools at all levels. We now see the results.

27. The CCP and the PLA carried Russia's brand of subversion to a new level. The CCP recruited American leaders and influencers at all levels almost at will via the internet, with flattery, grants, and by enlistment of our most renowned educators and scientists in the Chinese Thousand Talents Program. With Chinese grants, honoraria, and flattery, self-seeking Americans became unofficial Chinese operatives willingly and almost legally.

28. The PLA enrolled young officers in US universities at a graduate level where they had access to classified industrial and military research resulting in the wholesale theft of critical secret military and industrial data.

29. In 1999 two young Chinese colonels wrote an extensive outline of how China could defeat the United States avoiding direct military conflict while using every subversive means to destroy us. Their book *Unrestricted Warfare* followed the wisdom of Sun Tzu, a Chinese

general, strategist, writer, and philosopher 500 years BC, who in his book *The Art of War* wrote, "If one party is at war with another, and the other party does not realize it is at war, the party who knows it is at war almost always has the advantage and usually wins," The authors advocated waging a war on an adversary with methods so covert and seemingly so benign that the party being attacked does not realize it's being attacked.[2]

30. The CCP fully acknowledges its war, and views globalization as China's new world order.

31. Furthermore, China operates a highly technical, but deadly and evil forced organ transplant business. Modern laboratory and hospital facilities carry out extensive genomic tracing and typing of millions of political prisoners, providing a nearly limitless source of compatible donors for a profitable global trade in human organs.

32. The CCP attempts to indenture small South Pacific nations in a debt trap by building a highly mortgaged shipping port with a promise of prosperity and then foreclosing on the debt. China thus acquires strategic naval bases and shipping facilities.

---

[2] Qiao Liang, born 1955, a retired general in the PLA Air Force, military theorist, and author, the deputy director of the creative department of the PLAAF, the deputy secretary-general of the Council for National Security Policy Studies

Wang Xiangsui (王湘穗, born October 1, 1954), professor at Beihang University and a retired senior Colonel in the PLA

33. Legislators as puppets of both technocrats and oligarchs, and a flood of cash contributions from Chinese sources, targeted corporations and individuals for profit and control—contributing to Communism's desired level of subversion, control and destabilization.

34. Legislators unwittingly succumbed to CCP bribery, assignation, and marriage. Documented Chinese spy Christine Fang, "Fang Fang" with Representative Eric Swalwell (*Fang Fang Goes Bang Bang*, sic), is one of many such examples.

35. Unions seeking foreign membership embrace globalism at the expense of US workers.

36. The implementation of Communist subversion as practiced by Russia's KGB and later adopted by the CCP, follows four stages: It begins with 20 to 40 years of demoralization and propaganda. America has already traveled the antipatriotic route, and now we are living with radical prejudices, turning against ourselves. Destabilization emerges as the second stage with disruption of basic cultural and legal tenets. With extreme destabilization, riots and revolution emerge as the third-stage crisis, and when finally suppressed, a new final stage of normalization emerges that more closely aligns with Marxism and/or the unelected power structure (dialectic materialism) and the great reset.

37. Much of what we see today from either political perspective resembles the crisis stage of Communism's dialectic, their strategy for subversion, destruction, and takeover.

38. We see rioting, looting, arson, and a disregard for the law by perpetrators and leftist local governments alike. These are regressive, not progressive behaviors.

39. So who stands to benefit? An embedded bureaucracy, NGOs with foreign interests, oligarchs, officials on the take, unions seeking

international membership, "The Great Reset" of the World Bank, the World Economic Forum, the technocracy of Silicon Valley, multinationals outsourcing manufacturing and jobs, and the CCP, our communist adversaries. All masking as legitimate liberal politics seeking a more benevolent, equal, and Socialist society.

40. The Communist agenda of subversion, a political agenda for Socialism, a corporate agenda for cheap (even slave) labor, a banking agenda for profit from investment and capital flow, a union agenda for international unionization, an oligarch agenda for manipulation and control, a Silicon Valley technocracy agenda for Asian labor and outsourced fabrication, and legislators facilitating all of the above in exchange for enrichment and power. This varied cabal in unison demand deficit trade and globalization, the driving force of capital divergence, for their own self-interest. Never mind that all this was the CCP's strategy to cause the United States and the West to destroy themselves from within.

41. There appears to be evidence of subversion in the judiciary, FBI, the media, unions, the Teachers Union, colleges, and universities.

42. We teach hate, racism, and victimization in our schools. We criticize our Constitution, and teach a revised, shame-driven history of America in our schools. Hate is now epidemic and more contagious than Covid. You can't find humor on TV or in the movies—only the F word.

43. Legislators and elected officials find ways to manipulate the vote, perpetuating a lifetime in office, probably true of both parties, with corruption beyond gerrymandering.

44. Suspension of due process for political rivals. Were both political parties complicit in this practice or only the FBI? Did globalism lead to this sad judicial disintegration and disregard for our Constitution? Defund the police in Gotham City. What could be more destabilizing?

Sleeping with the enemy became the profitable and politically correct thing to do. All of these factors, including subversion, contributed to or resulted from globalization, and all of them undermine our democracy; they violate our laws and restructure our government into an authoritarian if not a totalitarian form no longer representative of the people and certainly not a democracy.

Peter Schweizer p(2022) in his book *Red Handed*, wrote:

"From the beginning of our republic, there have been deep concerns that foreign money and corruption would be used to buy off America's aristocracy." Alexander Hamilton, writing in the Federalist Papers, argued, "One of the weak sides of republics, among their numerous advantages, is that they afford too easy an inlet to foreign corruption." The Founders assumed that foreign rivals—especially Great Britain—would look for opportunities to weaken and divide us by striking deals with members of American high society. George Washington echoed those concerns in his farewell address, speaking of the "insidious wiles of foreign influence," which he considered "the most baneful foes of republican government." Likewise, James Madison was wary of foreign influence operating in the corridors of American politics and the business elite. "The public attention has been much employed for some time, on the danger of foreign influence," he wrote in 1799. "To be honorable to our character, and adequate to our safety, it ought to be pointed to every quarter where danger lurks, and most awake to that, from which danger is most to be feared." Madison believed the business elite were vulnerable because the British Crown had money to throw around: "Being an absolute monarchy in its executive department, [Britain] can distribute its money for secret services with every advantage of safety and success."

The fears for our republic of Alexander Hamilton, George Washington, and James Madison have become reality today, if one dares to look behind the political façade.

Remember the words Thomas Paine read to George Washington's troops before crossing the Delaware River on Christmas Day in a snowstorm, to surprise and rout the British army. The victory in Trenton turned the tide for American freedom. *The American Crisis* (1776): These are the times that try men's souls . . . Heaven knows how to put a proper price upon . . . freedom. Britain, with an army to enforce her tyranny, has declared that she has a right (not only to tax) but to bind us in all cases whatsoever . . . Even the expression is impious; for so unlimited a power can belong only to God."

Did the fictional *Star Trek* TV series add yet another avenue for teaching neoliberal political correctness to our youth? *Star Trek* economics: A back episode of *Star Trek* on YouTube promoting a new movie, shows the Star Ship *Enterprise* finding cryogenically frozen persons from the '60s. Upon recovery, one overbearing tycoon demands access to his brokerage accounts.

Captain Picard explains to the gentleman, "In the past three hundred years, people are no longer obsessed with things. The need for possessions grew out of our infancy."

"You got it all wrong. It has never been about possessions. It's about power," replied the time traveler.

"Power to do what?"

"To control your life, your destiny."

"That kind of control is an illusion."

"Really. I'm here, aren't I? I should be dead, but I'm not. Look what happened to us. There's no trace of my money. My office is gone. What will I do? How will I live?"

"This is the twenty-fourth century. Material needs no longer exist."

"Then what's the challenge?"

"The challenge, Mr. H, is to improve yourself, to enrich yourself."

Liberal globalism in the modern era promises socialism and, as of necessity, authoritative leadership. Why have young people so embraced the utopian scheme of globalism? Comic books defined the morality of previous generations. For the millennials, *Star Trek*'s futuristic utopia may be one answer, but in *Star Trek*'s 300-year future, war and evil still live.

Is what we are witnessing now, the realization of a theory known as the Fourth Turning (N. Howe & W. Strauss, 1997)? Will such a socialistic dream of equality and abundance as voiced by Captain Picard ever be possible? Or will our civilization go the way of others only to reemerge like China, or as a Chinese colony, or some other dystopian dictatorship? Or will the fourth turning be a turn away from the failed utopia of global citizenship and back to an embrace of our world's many civilizations?

During the Korean war, I was a survival instructor with a mission of teaching bomber crews how to survive in the Siberian Arctic, resist interrogation, escape, evade, and set up a viable means of communication and extraction from the Siberian tundra. It included recovery from one-way missions, part of the Strategic Air Command's war plan.

Once our downed American pilots were captured, North Korea transferred them to the Russians for interrogation. Russia moved these prisoners through the railhead at Khasan to the Russian interior for interrogation and brainwashing. Many were never seen again. The air force gave much thought to the adverse effects of brainwashing and the security risks that brainwashing presented. Some prisoners escaped. Others were eventually returned. What were the aftereffects and loyalties among those who were forced to endure cultural reeducation and experimental chemicals? These questions persisted after the war in Vietnam. How indelible will be the subversion of American youth and students throughout and after the Vietnam war?

The risks then and now arose from subversive education, corruption of popular culture and the media, the Jane Fonda phenomena. R. J. Lifton (1989) wrote an extensive study of these aftereffects, *Thought Reform and the Psychology of Totalism: A Study of "Brainwashing in China."* Lifton describes a quest for absolute or totalistic belief systems as a dangerous direction of the 20th century mind. He views this totalism as both political and religious leading to fundamentalism with "manipulation and exploitation of ordinary supplicants or recruits who form their idealism from below." Interestingly, Lifton offers species awareness as both a protection and a remedy. He observes that the totalistic mind set is in any case part of the human "repertoire" with an ever-present potential to manifest when conditions are right.

Yuri Bezmenov suggests that years of subversive demoralization creates just such conditions. Subversive propaganda, cultural reeducation, hate, and corruption from popular media persist today, as does Jane Fonda. Will the insanity go away once and if our nation returns to a more representative republic? Those who embrace the totalism of socialist ideology seem unlikely to change.

In *The Crisis of Democracy* (1975), a book derived from a report to the TLC outlining the growing problem with the governability of democracies, writers M. Crozier, S. P. Huntington, and J. Watanuki expanded their initial paper to full text, describing what they called increasing demands on government, and peoples' lack of compliance and cooperation with government. The tone trended to the authoritarian and supported an autocratic role for an unelected NGO seeking cooperation initially between Europe, Japan, and America, but soon included other nations with an elitist totalitarian view.

Multilateral trade at any cost for this elitist group left the United States with a minority vote from an international group dominating the cabinet of every administration until Trump. *The Crisis of Democracy* helped to define the "Deep State" and the totalitarian nature of globalization. This report and the book may still be the academic seed of an idea for a regressive governance to displace representative government by and for the people. Although the *Crisis of Democracy* questions the governability of a democracy, the book might better question democracy's ability to represent its people.

Love Letter to America, (T. Schuman [actually Yuri Bezmenov, KGB defector],1984) wrote of the four stages of Communist ideological subversion, and the ways in which such strategies cause an enemy to destroy itself from within.

As the United States devolved into the crisis-and-chaos stage of subversion. China bought political influence with American dollars. The CCP engaged in widespread espionage; it promoted globalization as its path to world trade and world domination. The Marxists were not alone in securing power and profit from the chaos, however.

Writing in 1992, C. Lash set forth *The Betrayal of Democracy* by a privileged class that's lost touch with Americans and the meaning of both democracy and citizenship. Lush's book, *The Revolt of the Elites,* posed the question in chapter 4, Does democracy deserve to survive? He paints a picture of the chaos, the decline of the middle class, of manufacturing, loss of jobs, the poor, rising crime, drugs, and decay of cities. He ends the chapter with the observation that democracy from the single-mindedly obsessed political views of racism and fanaticism can mean only one thing: "The defense of what they call cultural diversity."

Unrestricted Warfare: *China's Master Plan to Destroy America* (Qiao Lang, Wang Xiangsui, 1999, PLA Publishing House, Beijing) begins with an accurate appraisal of the US military, its strengths and weaknesses, including a detailed analysis of our Command-and-Control structure and our struggle against asymmetric warfare. The language and structure resemble those which one might hear in our own War College.

The authors refer to Sun Tzu's *Art of War* as the prototype for war without physical combat. From a quote by Oioa, "the first rule of unrestricted warfare is that there are no rules, with nothing forbidden." The book is not modest in outlining the extensive alternative weapons China intends to use against the West—especially the United States. It includes such diverse strategies as hacking, propaganda, bribery, economic overproduction, deception, theft, espionage, educational and ideological subversion, and geographic expansion like a game of GO—all of which begs the question, Was COVID19 a bioweapon? (p.18). If no other, this work is a must-read. The book is studied today in our military academies.

Plague of Corruption was written in 2020 by J. Mikovits and K. Heckenlively. Mikovits is the researcher who identified the mouse virus that contaminated early polio vaccines, causing chronic fatigue syndrome. She writes about the criminal assaults directed by big pharmaceutical companies to silence her. She lists the authoritarian interests who suppress free speech, free speculation, and the scientific method. The book shows the extent of corruption throughout our healthcare system and the way top-down authoritarianism, a byproduct and necessary feature of globalism as we see it, runs counter to science and leads to adverse consequences.

Mollie Ziegler Hemingway graduated from the University of Colorado with a degree in economics. Now an author, columnist, and political commentator, she is the editor in chief of the online magazine, *The Federalist*. The magazine inherits its passion for the Constitution from *The Federalist Papers*, a collection of 85 articles written by Alexander Hamilton, James Madison, and John Jay, promoting the ratification of our Constitution. Hemingway, in her new book *Rigged: How the Media, Big Tech and the Democrats Seized Our Elections* (2021), documents facts and the underlying corruption in the 2020 election. Dismissed as conspiracy theory by the Attorney General, FBI, the judiciary, and the media, the conspiracy theory has become well established in the published literature and thus in history. Mollie was there, a respected journalist. She documents corrupt behaviors of oligarchs, election officials, the media, and the FBI.

Batya Ungar-Sargo is an American journalist and deputy opinion editor of *Newsweek* magazine. Sargon also writes for The New York Times, Washington Post and Foreign Policy. In her book, *Bad News: How Woke Media Is Undermining Democracy*, (2021), she writes about present-day problems with the mainstream media. The first chapter alone on Pulitzer and his passion for writing for the people, makes the point of journalistic integrity. The author writes with a Dickensian eloquence. The book outlines the wealth, privilege, and education of today's young journalists who embrace racism and critical race theory while ignoring and belittling the working class and American people of all races. Wokeness—itself a derogatory defamation of speech—pleads for open borders and defunding of police, both to the detriment of those wokeness is said to protect. Ungar-Sargon pleads for journalists to return to Pulitzer's devotion to afflicting the powerful and protecting the afflicted. A chapter outlines the obscene wealth concentrated with the elite, indifferent to the resulting poverty of the working and consumer class. Batya paints a picture of class divide rather than racial divide. Hopefully this book will serve as an inflection point for journalistic integrity.

Rick Atkinson, an author of five books, worked as a newspaper reporter, editor, and foreign correspondent for *The Washington Post* before focusing on military history. Atkinson captures the frustration experienced by the colonists and their passion to be free of excess taxation and arbitrary authoritarian rule without civil liberties or ownership. His book, *The British are Coming: The War for America*, (2021), paints the revolution in meticulous detail, gives flesh to the history books and reads as a metaphor to our struggles today. The story comes as a kaleidoscope of historical letters, notes, and deeply researched history. The detail and trivia take on a life of their own. The vocabulary and idiom both voice the language of 1776 and the passion for freedom and self-rule. Not the whole story by any means, but Atkinson provides the reader with a living presence in the battles, failures, and successes through the summer, fall, and winter of 1776. He includes the words of Thomas Paine, read to the troops before Washington and a determined force of ragged men cross the Delaware River in a snowstorm on Christmas Day to surprise and defeat the British in the battle of Trenton. "These are the times that try men's souls . . ." Words not at all inappropriate for today's sad state of globalism and now war in Ukraine, not to mention taxes, inflation, censorship, propaganda, loss of due process, and arbitrary incarceration.

Victor Davis Hanson teaches military history, ancient warfare, and the classics at Stanford University's Hoover Institution. He is a professor emeritus at California State University, and a frequent visiting professor at Hillsdale College. His book, *The Dying Citizen* (2021), traces citizenship from ancient Greece through its rare appearance through history and around the world. Today, citizenship exists only in the Western democracies. Hanson holds the middle class as the driving force of citizenship. "Without a middle class," the author says, "a society becomes bifurcated. Society splinters into ones of modern masters and peasants. The role of government no longer ensures freedom but provides for the poor and exempts the wealthy who in turn enrich and empower the governing class."

R. F. Kennedy Jr, son of Bobby Kennedy, is as liberal as they come. A Harvard graduate and environmental lawyer, with an economics degree from the London School of Economics, and a JD from the University of Virginia, Kennedy founded in 1999, and still directs the Water Keeper Alliance. Yet, Wikipedia calls him an author known for anti-vaccine propaganda and conspiracy theories. Kennedy actually writes more about the corruption between Big Pharmacology and government agencies, not just during the pandemic, but extending back to experimental drug treatments in Africa for TB, malaria, AIDS, and polio. His book, *The Real Anthony Fauci, Bill Gates, Big Pharma and the War on Democracy and Public Health* (2021) levels harsh criticism at what Kennedy sees as sloppy, corrupt, and self-serving science. Whether true or not, his doubts deserve further scientific inquiry. Neither profit nor politics serve either science or patient care.

United States of Fear by M. McDonald, MD (2021), calls further attention to the bureaucratic dictation of patient care during the pandemic for obvious personal and drug company gain, as though the patient did not know or the physician could not deviate from bureaucratic guidelines. McDonald tells the history of Big Pharma's abuse and the struggle physicians have with so-called evidence-based guidelines and politicization of medicine. McDonald calls the fearmongering of politics and greed a mass delusional psychosis. His psychiatric practice and years as an analyst support his diagnosis. "Adopting a world view that rejects and attacks reality is psychotic."

The illusion of evidence-based medicine, a recent opinion in the prestigious *British Medical Journal* (2022;376:o702) by J. Jureidini and L.B. McHenry states, "Evidence-based medicine has been corrupted by corporate interests, failed regulation, and commercialization of academia."

Peter Schweizer in his book *Red Handed* (2022), bravely outlines the extent to which the CCP and the PLA seduced the Washington elite and many others throughout America. The elite followed willingly the siren call for unlimited wealth and adulation.

Schweizer outlines the double-dipping of many legislators, who in retirement become highly paid lobbyists for China and more directly the CCP. He describes how cabinet members, diplomats, and even retired military engage in the same consulting businesses that initially in the '60s sought engagement, trade, and peace, but soon turned to vicious subversion.

For the Silicon Valley technocracy, the market opportunity for sales to China's 1.44 billion population was an irresistible siren call above all other considerations, and for most of these corporations, the profits outweighed any thoughts of national security. The author includes Wall Street's financing of the Chinese military, with investment products not accountable to our Securities Exchange Commission, including many retirement funds.

Schweizer goes on to describe the Bush and Trudeau families' close relations with Chinese officials of the CCP. Don't forget Senator D. Feinstein or Senator M. McConnell and the Chao family of ship builders. Schweizer focuses particularly on Yale University with the massive and mostly unaccounted-for Chinese donations and joint programs. This book names names, dates, and dollar amounts with a surprisingly long list of persons whose greed forgoes their honor. He names a few not so easily seduced.

His last chapter makes suggestions: Ban lobbying on behalf of Chinese military- and intelligence-linked companies. Ban Chinese military- and intelligence-linked companies from appearing on US stock exchanges. Ban joint research between Chinese and American universities. Ban investment in corporations with Chinese military and intelligence projects. Schweizer suggests that Wall Street firms need to consistently apply environmental, social, and governance (ESG), SEC standards and national security to all Chinese investments.

Truth remains a challenge for Main Street media owned or financed by China. The CCP owns Hollywood as well.

James Mann is the former Beijing bureau chief for *The Los Angeles Times* and is now a scholar at Johns Hopkins University. He argues that "engagement" is essentially a strategic fraud. Clyde Prestowitz, a longtime observer and author on Chinese matters, believes that we should replace engagement with reciprocity. (However, reciprocity cannot exist when one party holds deception as the highest good while the other views truth as the guiding virtue—the Eastern mind set versus the West.)

Schweizer mentions the unlikely but hoped-for agreement between Ted Cruz (R) of Texas and Chuck Schumer (D) of New York in upholding the 1938 Foreign Agents Registration Act (FARA) and the 1966–2019 Foreign Contributions and Things of Value Act [§ 30121 & 303(2)]. Schweizer seems to endorse Prestowitz's view of "reciprocity in lieu of engagement," and our hope for further agreement between Cruz and Schumer in closing the loopholes. In any case we must counter Beijing's "elite capture strategy."

Education continues to subvert with political ideology. Universities censor free speech and civil discourse. We no longer teach ethics, western virtues, discipline, logic, or civility. Alana Mastrangelo, writing for Breitbart, reports: "Nearly 120 woke Yale Law School students disrupted a bipartisan panel about civil liberties last week by trying to shout down and intimidate the speakers—primarily attacking a speaker from Alliance Defending Freedom (ADF)—who had to be escorted out of the building by police. One of America's best and brightest future Ivy League graduates screeched at the ADF representative: "I will literally fight you, bitch!"

The crisis is now. Ever since Vietnam, our political system and shadow government have waged and continue to wage "unrestricted war." Not Democrat against Republican, although that appears most visible, but globalist against nationalist. If America and the Constitution win, a wall of hatred will remain, much like the post–Civil War reconstruction. Both political parties might be forgiven because their humanitarian goals were hijacked by Globalization. Any post-Ukraine reconstruction will of necessity require great leadership from both parties. Democrats, however, no longer have an Andrew Jackson to lead a reconstruction or an academic renaissance. Mending our way to a cooperative post globalist and postwar era will be challenging. It will require generations of education and civility to overcome decades of hate and chaos.

The United States placed sanctions against Russia because of Russia's invasion of Ukraine. Putin attempts to put the ruble on the gold standard. Russia's Central Bank will buy gold at 5000 rubles per gram. That strategy effectively undermines the US dollar. Inflation now reaches double digits. The World Economic Forum (WEF)with Klaus Schwab seeks a world currency, either digital or crypto, thus giving access to the activity and spending of every individual, to a vague international banking elite. Crypto currency includes a database that governments can access. The future of artificial intelligence (AI) uses a database to record all your activities. The Secret Service today announced the confiscation of vast sums of crypto currency involved in money laundering. Canada already demonstrated a willingness to confiscate bank accounts of truckers and the funds of those contributing to them. Schwab at the WEF suggests AI will become a further means of controlling the ungovernable, further advancing the agenda of the globalists. The internationalistic thinkers of Davos, K. Georgieva, Bulgarian economist and managing director of the International Monetary Fund (IMF), and C. Lagard, president of the European Central Bank still voice support for globalism and centralization.

What's going to happen? What's the conclusion? The outcome of the not-so-cold war between China, Russia, Iran, and North Korea and the West remains in doubt. The political war between neoliberal globalization and democracy continues. The Four Horsemen of the Apocalypse offer a view. Destruction rode in with the rioting, looting, arson, and political foul play. Putin's invasion of Ukraine brought us war and pestilence as did the COVID19 Wuhan pandemic. Famine could well follow.

Decades of Cold War with Russia now includes China, Iran and don't forget North Korea. While Ukraine becomes a hot foreign war, our domestic Cold War between globalization and democracy heats up, but still evades clarity, recognition and debate.

If we listen to R. Dalio, a major depression may last for a decade. Worse yet, a refusal of either political party to accept the outcome of 2022 or 2024 elections might result in open revolution. Dalio refers to the history of populism and revolution. He points to historical conditions like today's, suggesting that populists on both sides are fighters and that civil war could emerge. I trust not.

Any assessment deserves a plan. Inflation presents today's greatest problem. The Federal Reserve attempted to control inflation with progressively higher interest rates. Austerity and high interest rates as the only solution hurts more than it helps. Soon we'll be driving 55 mph again. Politicians attempt to reduce the debt through inflation and that only hurts the people's wealth.

The economists at the Federal Reserve need to find a way to stimulate the velocity multiple in the Gross Domestic Product equation. GDP = velocity x money supply. Stop restrictions on energy. Promote American business. Enterprise, innovation and marginal-return will do more to curtail CO_2 emissions than government edit. American business velocity will do more to stop inflation than interest rates. (Velocity and GDP are not equally shared in society. Velocity lives with the middle class while GDP and M2 enrich with the wealthy.)

Stop deficit trade to increase domestic velocity. We stress this fact again and again in the economics above. The strategy comes back to the macroeconomic sectoral balances. Every purchase of a foreign made product amounts to a positive entry to the local velocity of the nation of origin and a negative entry to our own local velocity. Velocity as we show here has a far greater effect on the Gross Domestic Product than (M1). Follow the money. Building local velocity will reverse the drain of liquidity from the small business and demand side of the market. In doing so, the market activity, of necessity, must increase—a far greater effect on the economy and checking inflation than overall money supply (M1). Furthermore, increased productivity will swallow inflation. Market productivity dominates. That's the magic of American capitalism.

Political polarization and traditional battles between Democrat and Republican fail to address the far more relevant war between Globalist and Constitutionalist, between globalization and democracy. The battle lines need better definition and publicity. If the vail of blindness can be lifted, our Constitution might yet prevail. Optimistically, we may yet extract ourselves from the new world disorder and reclaim our Democracy. Lift the blindness of post Vietnam political correctness and reverse the disintegration of our Republic. Look to the future to understand the past. We'll see what happens.

GDP and Money Supply (M1) in trillions

Date	GDP t	M1 t	Velocity
2021	22.06	20.35	1.18
2020	20.89	17.81	1.17
2019	21.54	3.9231	5.46
2018	20.61	3.7277	5.53
2017	19.39	3.5640	5.44
2016	16.49	3.2446	5.08
2015	16.47	3.0730	5.33
2014	16.15	2.9212	5.53
2013	15.76	2.6414	5.97
2012	15.38	2.4586	6.26
2011	15.19	2.1618	7.03
2010	14.94	1.8600	8.03
2009	14.54	1.6965	8.57
2008	14.58	1.6034	9.09
2007	14.99	1.3711	10.93
2006	14.72	1.3849	10.63

Note the dramatic increase in money supply from 2019 to 2021 and the drop-off of velocity from 2007 to 2021. Figures are not exact and were previously hard to find. St Louis Fed now publish both M1 and Velocity. 2021 GDP is an estimate. Note the pandemic effect in 2020 and 2021. Velocity reflects productivity, income, morale, and energy. It's the churn within the market economy.

POSTSCRIPT

Halfway through the thirteenth editing of my book *Globalization or Democracy*, I found Yuri Alexandrovich Bezmenov's (1939-1993) lecture discussing his KGB defection on YouTube. Also known as Thomas David Schuman, Bezmenov had defected to Canada with the assistance of the CIA in 1970. The effect on me was chilling. I had not thought about Russian espionage in nearly 70 years. Watching Bezmenov lecture on Russian subversion catapulted me back to my own time in the Korean War, dealing with survival and intelligence in what was, back then, the Strategic Air Command.

During the writing of *Globalization or Democracy*, it had already become objectively evident to me that globalism in its present form was destroying both our democracy and our economy. The role of the CCP in this subversion had also become clear as I explored the evidence. How foolish had I been to have naively assumed Russia's long-standing subversion and propaganda were a long-forgotten thing of the past? Bezmenov's lecture on Communist subversion, euphemistically called "active measures" with their apparently high success rate had come as a definite wakeup call.

The current degree of political polarization with its seemingly inexplicable level of hate and complete absence of humor now raging in our country suddenly made sense. Furthermore, so did the fact that those embracing the hate, with its forbidding conflict and confrontation, seemed incapable of acknowledging the hard facts and evidence right before their eyes.

Suddenly, like millions of other veterans, I could see the rejection of American institutions had begun with things such as the rioting at the end of the war in Vietnam. What had been less evident, though, was the KGB's role in the continuance of this ideological subversion.

After studying political science at the University of Toronto, Bezmenov had worked for the Canadian Broadcasting Corporation in Montreal, where he had done freelance writing under the alias of Thomas Schuman. Whether due to Russian threats or for other unknown reasons, he eventually moved to Los Angeles.

In 1984, Yuri Bezmenov gave an interview with Edward Griffin titled, Soviet Subversion of the World Free Press. As the YouTube video outlined in clear and graphic terms, 85% of the KGB budget had been directed towards disinformation and ideological subversion. During this interview with Edward Griffin, Bezmenov cited the outstanding success rate subversion tactics had generated in country after country, clearly demonstrating how Russia even today continues to sow ideological subversion within the US and the West.

In his video, Bezmenov describes the long timeline of Russia's four strategies of subversion—a concept that now seems to fit like a glove in viewing the destabilization evolving in the US since the Vietnam War.

Demoralization is a 20-year program to reeducate and brainwash a generation of youth, followed by Destabilization, as evidenced by the Vietnam protesters having become teachers and legislators who now question the meaning of equality, our Constitution, capitalism, and even morality.

The third stage, Crisis, is in full play in the United States right now with rioting, looting and chaos in the streets, heralding a complete breakdown of law and order in our country.

And, if all goes according to plan, the fourth stage, Normalization, will soon follow. Normalization, where socialism is accepted as the alternative to war, civil war, or revolution—Marxism deftly ushered in by today's Chinese Communist Party with its vanguards of regimentation, equality, mind control, and dystopia—all at the cost of freedom.

Every American and every high school student should listen to Yuri Brezmenov's lecture. His words stand as a dire warning and are as prophetic today as were the writings of English American revolutionist and political activist Thomas Paine (1737-1809).

In his video, Brezmenov claims it takes 20 years to brainwash a generation of students to the point of destabilization. Notably, Russia has engaged in its own effort to corrupt our education system and further racial conflict for more like 70 years, undermining American values—not just education, but political, legislative, cultural, religious, legal, and even military—by sowing conflict and discord wherever it could along the way.

How alarming then that the Peoples Liberation Army and the Chinese Communist Party appear to be far more efficient at subversion than the KGB or today's SVR-RF (Sluzhba vneshney razvedki Rossiyskoy Federatsii). The Chinese accomplished destabilization in a much shorter time, doing far more damage than Brezmenov could ever have foreseen.

With their takeover of globalization, the worldwide release of the Coronavirus and infiltration of all elements of our society—according to Christopher Wray, Director of the FBI—China and its PLA are now a far greater threat to America than Russia. With infiltration of the US media and more sleepers, the PLA operatives financially compromised US leadership from the top right down to the local level.

If we look at the level of hatred within America as a measure of the subversion, we find it everywhere. There are no simple political issues anymore. Both sides seem radicalized to one degree or another. Conflict,

145

stimulating rage against ourselves, was the Communist goal. It does not matter the subject. The dour cloak of hatred dominates media, schools, legislature, and now the street—a Marxist's wet dream.

Bezmenov visited his former wife and children in Montréal in 1993. The official cause of his death two weeks later was a "massive heart attack."

Interestingly, Bezmenov's lecture and books are now being studied by the Joint Special Operations University (JSOU), the University of Pennsylvania's Biden Center for Diplomacy and Global Engagement. They are also being studied by Michael Carpenter, former deputy Assistant Secretary of Defense, and by Yale professor Asha Rangappa, and have now reemerged on YouTube.

Bezmenov's books include: *No Novosti Is Good News, World Thought Police, Black Is Beautiful, Communism Is Not.* In Yuri's book, *Love Letter to America* 1984, Brezmenov suggests it will take 20 years to reeducate a new generation of youth and to ferret out the sleepers and financially compromised supporters of Communist normalization. I would add to that list the need for a reeducation in citizenship, understanding the Constitution, and humor.

APPENDIX

Timeline of events that contributed to a culture of globalization far more complex than free trade.

1648	Peace of Westphalia, beginning of Western international law
1776	Adam Smith Wealth of Nations
1880	Arnold Toynbee "Industrial Revolution, a fixation of wealth and a rise of poverty."
1934-61	Arnold Joseph Toynbee (nephew) Civilization on Trial, The Prospects for Western Civilization, The Economy of the Western Hemisphere and Why Nations Fail—the origins of power prosperity and poverty.
1921	Council on Foreign Relations (CFR) long history, League of Nations, UN etc.
1947	Republic of China publishes a map showing an 11-line, later the 9-line, justifying its claim of the South China Sea
1951	Treaty of Paris establishing the Coal and Steel Community (ECSC) and the early foundations of the European Union.
6/1950	North Korean invasion of South Korea, unresolved
10/1950	Chinese troops crossed the Yalu River
3/1953	Joseph Stalin Dies
1953-1961	Eisenhower pres. With JF Dulles Sec. of State

7/1953	Armistice Korea
5/1954	Dien Bien Phu Geneva Accord divides Vietnam
1959-1975	War in Vietnam; US enters '64; Russia supports NK
1956	Egypt nationalizing the Suez Canal, a landmark in the slow death of colonialism
1957	The Treaty of Rome forming a European economic community (EEC) and, independently, the European Atomic Energy Community (EAEC).
1961-1963	John F Kennedy, Dean Rusk Sec. State
1963-1969	LBJ, Dean Rusk
1967	ECSC, EEC and EAEC merging, solidifying the European Union
1968	Peak anti-Vietnam War protests, student occupation of administrative offices, and rejection of traditional American institutions.
1969-	1974 Nixon, Kissinger replaces Rogers Sec of State
1969	Brzezinski's globalization speech
8/1971	Nixon ends the gold standard
1971	Kissinger visits China
2/1972	Nixon visits China
7/1972	Jane Fonda to Hanoi; massive US student anti- Vietnam riots
1970	CFR publication of first FP magazine
1973	Denmark, Ireland, and UK joining the EU
7/1973	Carter, Rockefeller, Brzezinski form Trilateral Commission

8/74	Nixon resigns
1974-1977	Ford pres. with Rockefeller VP and Kissinger SS
1977-1981	Carter with Vance Sec St and Brzezinski NSA
1977	Imported oil made trade deficits mushroom
1979	Diplomatic relations established with China
1983	Police action Grenada
1986	Single-Europe-Act and the addition of Portugal and Spain to the EU
1989	Destruction of Berlin Wall and collapse of Russian economy
1990	Neoconservatism, concept of a New World Order advanced by President George H. Bush
1990	Iraq, Desert Storm; President George H. Bush
1992-1995	Bosnian War
1993-2001	Bill Clinton with Christopher then Albright Sec St
1993	NAFTA
1996	China temporary Most Favored Nation
2001	9/11
2001	10/7 Afghanistan
2001	Joseph E. Stiglitz Nobel Prize for information, the markets and globalization
2001	China's most favored nation, MFN, status made permanent
2003	Iraq War II, George W. Bush

2011	China reassertion of its "indisputable sovereignty" over the South China Sea, reaffirming the 9 dash line
2014	Russia's annexation of Crimea
2016	Brexit, Prime Minister Theresa May
2016	Wave of nationalism /populism rejecting unfair trade, job loss, manufacturing loss, uncontrolled immigration, fruitless foreign wars, election of Donald Trump, President (note: former members of the Trilateral Commission ejected from all levels of the administration, severe backlash)
2018	Putin and Xi Jinping summit meeting to counterbalance US unilateralism
2019	Davos, Switzerland, World Economic Forum Xi Jinping celebrating globalization as the wave of the future, laying out China's strategy to extend globalization worldwide and China's plan for the future with its beltway construction, control of seaports, 5G, artificial intelligence, AI, and dominance in world manufacturing
2019	25% tariffs on China and a ban on Huawei Technologies due to security issues, the theft of personal and intellectual data, Chinese military ownership and history of hacking
2020	COVID19, contested presidential election, massive increase in M2
2021	Restrictions on US oil production, Pandemic lockdown
2/16/22	Trudeau evokes emergency powers, confiscates bank accounts / truckers demonstration
2/23/22	Putin invades Ukraine, gold standard for oil

2022   Inflation, increasing interest rates, recession

2022   Emerging corruption, censorship, propaganda

REFERENCES

Bastiampillai, T., FRANZCP1,2; Sharfstein, S. S. , MD3; & Allison, S.,
     FRANZCP2 "Increase in US Suicide Rates and the Critical
     Decline in Psychiatric Beds" JAMA. Published online
     November 3, 2016. doi:10.1001/jama.2016.16989

Brill, S., *Tailspin*

Clemens, M. A., & Williamson, J. G., "A Tariff-Growth-Paradox," NBER
     working paper Sep 2001

Dalio, R. (2018). "Big Debt Crisis" recent interviews CNBC

Dertouzos, M. l, Lester, R. K., & Solow, R. M., *Made in America*, ISBN 0-
     262-04100-6

Freedman, M., (1956, 1963). The Theory of Consumption Function,
     Capitalism and Freedom, Quantitative Theory of Money,
     Momentary History of the United States

George, H. (1879). *Progress and Poverty*

Greenspan, A. *The Age of Turbulence*, ISBN978-1-59420-131-8

Hanson, V. D., Fields Without Dreams and The Case for Trump

Hayek, F. A, *Individualism and Economic Order*, various essays, ISBN 0-
     226-32093-6

Ise, J., *Sod and Stubble*, ISBN 0-8082-5098-3 and (1946) *Economics* Harper & Bros.

Jones-Smith, JC, "Obesity and the Food Environment," *Diabetes Care* 2013

Kelly, K., *Rules for the New Economy*, ISBN 0-670-88111-2

Keynes, J. M., (1936). The General Theory of Employment Interest and Money

Krugman, P., The Return of Depression Economics, ISBN 978-0-393-07101-6; (2009). The Return of Depression Economics, WW Norton NY; (2020) Arguing with Zombies

Liang, Q. & Xiangsui, W., *Unrestricted Warfare*, PLA Literature and Arts Publishing House

Mac Donald, H., *The Diversity Delusion*, St Martin's Press

Mackey, J. & Sisodia, R., *Conscious Capitalism*, ISBN 978-1-4221-4420-6

Mackintosh, J. "What Modern Monetary Theory Gets Right and Wrong." WSJ 20190402

Malthus, T. R., (1798). *Principles of Population.* London

Mandelbrot, B., & Hudson, R.L. *The Misbehavior of Markets.* ISBN 0-45-04355-0

McCann, B., "Institutional Investor" Oct 19, 2015 Hedge Funds Smell Blood in the Student Debt Market,

Orwell, G. *1984*

Paine, T., Common Sense, Rights of Man, Agrarian Justice, American Crisis, The Age of Reason

Piketty, T., *CAPITAL in the Twenty-First Century*, ISBN 978-0+674-43000-6, 2020, *Capital and Ideology*, Harvard University Press, translation by Arthur Goldhammer

Plato. (360 BC). *Republic*, Book VIII,

Robinson, *Why Nations Fail* ISBN 978-0-307-71923-2

Sachs, J. D. *Common Wealth*, ISBN 978-1-59420-127-1

Smith, A., (1776-1790). Wealth of Nations; (1759-1790). The Theory of Moral Sentiments, George Soros on Globalization Public Affairs, NY, 2002

Spalding, R., *Stealth War*. Penguin 2019

Stiglitz, J. E., Making Globalization Work, Globalization and Its Discontents

Toynbee, A., "Lectures on the Industrial Revolution"

Toynbee, A. J., A Study of History, Civilization on Trial, Prospects for Western Civilization, The Economics of the Western Hemisphere, Why Nations Fail, https://www.uscc.gov/sites/default/files/Chinese%20Companies%20on%20U.S.%20Stock20Exchanges.pdf

Woolf, S., "Life expectancy and Mortality Rates US 1959-2017." JAMA Nov 26, 2019, vol. 322, #20

END NOTES AND CITATIONS

[1] House.gov always and Means TPP, Japan & US side by side 2012

[2] M Levinson Feb 21, 2018 Congressional Research Service

[3] Brookings Institution July 10, 2018

[4] ITi Manufacturing News, Mike Stewart Mar 9, 2017 and October 17, 2014

[5] Stiller Center for Economic Studies, Pro Market Blog, Christoph Boehm & Nitya Podalai-Nayar University of Chicago Jul 11, 2019 and University of Michigan Feb 2017

[6] How the Decline in Community Banks Has Hurt US Entrepreneurship, Barron's 20190518

[7] Qiao Liang & Wang Xiangsui, Unrestricted Warfare, PLA Literature and Arts Publishing House

[8] https://www.antiwar.com/berkman/trilat.html, http://trilateral.org/page/3/about-trilateral, https://en.m.wikipedia.org/wiki/Trilateral_Commission, https://canadafreepress.com/article/flashback-the-domination-of-barack-obama-by-the-trilateral-commission

[9] Daily Treasury Statement: http://www.fsapps.fiscal.treasury.gov

[10] John Ise, PhD, LLB, 1885-1969, professor of economics University of Kansas, 1920-1955 past president AEA, *Economics,* Harper & Brothers 1946

[11] Nominal GDP and M1 variously reported by BEA, The Balance, and World Bank for estimate of velocity only

[12] https://www.investopedia.com/articles/personal-finance/050615/are-you-top-one-percent-world.asp

[13] https://www.bea.gov/system/files/2019-05/Distributional-Financial-Accounts.pdf

[14] Krugman, Paul. *Arguing with Zombies:* Economics, Politics, and the Fight for a Better Future (p. 253). W. W. Norton & Company

[15] *Macro Economics*, Wayne Godley, T Francis Cripps, 1983, British economist formula for financial and sectoral balances

[16] Piketty, *Capital*

[17] US Bureau of Economic Analysis

[18] Arnold Toynbee, Lectures on the Industrial Revolution, 1884

[19] US Is Learning That China Likes Its Own Model As China's economy and global reach expand, it doesn't feel the need to adapt for Western acceptance. Gerald F. Seib May 27, 2019 9:46 a.m. ET https://www.wsj.com/articles/u-s-is-learning-that-china-likes-its-own-model-11558964778?reflink=share_mobilewebshare

[20] 5G is the 5th generation mobile network. It is a new global wireless standard after 1G, 2G, 3G, and 4G networks. 5G enables a new kind of network that is designed to connect virtually everyone and everything together including machines, objects, and devices

[21] Xi Jinping's speech in Davos, Switzerland WEF https://www.diamandis.com/blog/china-next-tech-superpower https://america.cgtn.com/2017/01/17/full-text-of-xi-jinping-keynote-at-the-world-economic-forum

[22] *The Real Adam Smith*, Johan Norberg, a video on YouTube and Amazon, http://www.gstatic.com/tv/thumb/tvbanners/12618469/p12618469_b_v8_aa.jpg

[23] Bridging Adam Smith's *Theory of Moral Sentiments* and *Wealth of Nations* John Dwyer, "Journal of British Studies" Oct 2005, pp-662-687

[24] Journal of British Studies vol 44 #4, Bridging Adam Smith's *Theory of Moral Sentiments* and *Wealth of Nations,* John Dwyer, Oct 2005 pp 662-687

[25] For instance, given the share of income from capital as 6 times National Income, equivalent to 6 years of National Income, expressed as β or 600%; then, given a return on capital (r) of 5 percent, the return on capital investments (a) will equal 30 percent of National Income. a = r x β. -

Piketty offers a second equation: β = savings divided by growth, s/g; 6 = 12/2 where a savings of 12 percent divided by a growth rate of the economy of only 2 percent results in a capital income ratio of 6 years of National Income. Apparently, a long-term reality not always evident in the short or midterm. (The equation can also suggest growth rate in terms of the savings rate divided by the capital income ratio, not as a cause and effect but with an increased savings reflected by greater growth and a more vibrant economy).

[26] Ray Dalio, *Big Debt Crisis 2018*, founder of Bridgewater Investments

[27] https://www.economy.com/united-states/nominal-fixed-investment-gross-fixed-capital-formation Moody's Analytics Nominal fixed investment, gross fixed capital Q3 2019

[28] Reuters Business News Dec 31, 2018 Sujata Rao & Ritvik Carvallio

[29] Annual Review of Economics, Global Wealth Inequality, Gabriel Zucman1, Department of Economics, University of California, National Bureau of Economic Research, Cambridge, MA

[30] Understanding the Modern Monetary System, Cullen Roche, **Error! Hyperlink reference not valid.**s-i-g-t-x-mhttp://www.pragcap.com/my-view-on-mmt/

[31] AMA Journal Maternal-Infant Dyad Disconnect, Sarah Handley, M.D. Sindhi Srinivas, M.D. Scott Lorch, M.D. Aug 13, 2019, vol 322, #6

[32] Life Expectancy US 1959-2017, Steven Woolf, MD, Heidi Schoomaker, MA, NEJM vol 322 #20

[33] http://clinicaldiagnosis.blogspot.com/2014/02/global-burden-of-disease-study-gbd.html

[34] VR Fuchs Jama, 2013- jamanetwork.com

[35] Kelly Young NEJM First Watch 10/12/19

[36] Thomas Sydenham, 1624-1689. And others sought additional knowledge in foreign medical schools; a surprising number of these historically great physicians in addition translated Hippocrates and, most intriguingly, suffered from the gout.

[37] Office of Natural Drug Control Policy, ONDCP, Marina-Armada de Mexico, 24/08/2019, Port of Lazaro Cardenas, Michoacán, MX

[38] Fentanyl is a synthetic opioid pain reliever used for severe pain and cancer, 100 times as potent as morphine. Illegal fentanyl is often added to

or cut with heroin or cocaine. It is easily manufactured in analogs to increase potency and avoid schedule 1 listing. Much of it is manufactured in China and shipped along with other goods or in US mail. https://www.cdc.gov/drugoverdose/opioids/fentanyl.html

[39]

http://forestmanagement.enr.gov.nt.ca/forest_education/amazing_tree_fa cts.htm

[40] https://www.eia.gov/todayinenergy/detail.php?id=39992

[41] Lukasik, Stephen J. (2011). "Why the Arpanet Was Built". IEEE Annals of the History of Computing. 33 (3): 4–20. doi:10.1109/MAHC.2010.11 "Paul Baran and the Origins of the Internet". RAND corporation. Retrieved March 29, 2011. Paul Baran (1960). "Reliable Digital Communications Systems Using Unreliable Network Repeater Nodes". RAND Corporation papers

[42] *Unrestricted Warfare*, published Feb 1999, Oiao Lang and Wang Xiangsui PLA Airforce, and required reading US Naval Academy

[43] *The Art of War*, Sun Tzu, New Translation, R.L. Wing, Doubleday NY, 1988

[44] Kyle Bass, Steve Bannon, interview YouTube; Robert Spalding, *Stealth War;* Penguin 2019

[45] https://www.theatlantic.com/politics/archive/2019/08/inside-us-china-espionage-war/595747/

[46] DoD technical report, 17-10, Aug, 2017 PERSEREC Katherine L. Herbig, PhD

[47] No mention of China by name; also, the table of contents lists globalization on page 78. Reading p. 78 and adjacent pages, no mention of globalization, suggesting that the article was redacted

[48] Professor John Ise, PhD, LLB, KU, *Economics,* chapter 25, Harper Bros. 1946

[49] The return of Depression Economics, Paul Krugman

[50] Unproven and based on confidential inside information from the top management

[51] A Tariff- Growth Paradox, Michael A Clemens, Jeffery G Williamson, Dep Econ Harvard U, National Bureau of Economic Research, Sep 2001

[52] *Unrestricted Warfare*: China's Plan to Destroy America, Liang Qiao & Xiangsui Wang, PLA publishing & Shadow Lawn Press 2017

[53] Victor Davis Hanson "The Ancient Greeks and Western Civilization" multiple academic lectures

[54] Managing Director, Human Resources, and Chairman of the ethics committee of the WTO are members of the Chinese Communist Party, CCP. Kyle Bass CNBC Television 12/4/2019.

[55] Trilateral Commission, Senator Berry Goldwater, paperback, *With No Apologies,* a skillful, coordinated effort to seize control.

[56] Khasan, on the 11-mile Russian border with North Korea. (View from Google maps) Trans-Siberian RR connects directly with Pyongyang through Khasan. Russia vulnerable to Chinese expansionism across the 2,615.5-mile Sino-Russian border. Khasan was strategic key in Korean War and remains so today.

[57] Investigation: Why is China on the move in the South Pacific? 60 Minutes Australia, 17Nov19

[58] Sectoral balances https://en.wikipedia.org/wiki/Sectoral_balances

[59] Probably an oversimplification, personal investing I and government spending were not counted; an increase in either should be positive for consumers. and these results do support this sectoral analysis equation.

[60] www.fairus.org fact sheet 2019

[61] Forbes, Rebecca Fannin, US Investors Own a Piece of China Oct 29, 2019, 207 billion USD

[62] https://www.chinaorganharvest.org

[63] News.law.fordham.edu A Brief History of Tariffs

[64] Oct 2019 WWW.wotldmeters.info, China

[65] https://www.businessinsider.com/china-uighur-prison-camp-suspected-locations-maps-2019-11

[66] [sic] other people's wealth

[67] Read again the first three sentences of Adam Smith's *The Wealth of Nations*

[68] *Sophistical Refutations,* Aristotle, https://en.wikipedia.org/wiki/Sophistical_Refutations

[69] Bill Gates carbon sequestration project, Pinnacle Digest 28 Jun 2019

[70] Victor Davis Hanson (born September 5, 1953) is an American classicist, military historian, columnist, and farmer. He has been a commentator on modern and ancient warfare and contemporary politics

CPSIA information can be obtained
at www.ICGtesting.com
Printed in the USA
BVHW031135061022
648823BV00017B/831

9 781088 059357